Johannes de Alta Silva

Dolopathos

medieval & renaissance texts & studies

1. Frank Livingstone Huntley, *Bishop Joseph Hall and Protestant Meditation in Seventeenth-Century England: A Study, With the Texts of The Art of Divine Meditation (1606) and Occasional Meditations (1633).*

2. *Johannes de Alta Silva, Dolopathos: or The King and the Seven Wise Men.* Translated by Brady B. Gilleland.

3. Albert Rabil, Jr., *Laura Cereta: Quattrocento Humanist.*

Johannes de Alta Silva

Dolopathos

or

The King and the

Seven Wise Men

Translated by

Brady B. Gilleland

medieval & renaissance texts & studies
Center for Medieval & Early Renaissance Studies
BINGHAMTON, NEW YORK
1981

A grant from the Kent Memorial Fund
assisted in defraying the publication costs of this volume.

*This book is published in both
clothbound and paperbound editions.*

ISBN 0-86698-001-6 *(cloth)*
ISBN 0-86698-006-7 *(paper)*

Contents

Professor Peter K. Marshall of Amherst College went over the translation with a careful eye for both accuracy and fine shades of meaning. I am deeply grateful to him for his generous help.

B.B.G.

Introduction

The Author and the Story

ALL THAT WE KNOW of Johannes de Alta Silva comes from his only work, *Dolopathos, or The King and the Seven Wise Men*. He was a Cistercian monk in the monastery of Haute Seille (Alta Silva). From 1184 to 1212, this monastery was in the diocese of Bertrand, Bishop of Metz, to whom the work was dedicated; hence, it has been variously placed between these dates.[1] There is also a later version of the work, an adaptation by a French poet and trouvere named Herbert, who lived at the court of King Philipp August and wrote sometime during the first quarter of the thirteenth century.[2] Herbert's work is not a complete and accurate translation of John's *Dolopathos* but has some variations which show that the poet is using another source or sources, and that he is not relying upon John's work alone.[3]

Dolopathos is a work of prose fiction, consisting of the dedication to Bertrand, a preface, a frame story, and a series of tales. The preface asserts that the work will be a true history about the life of a mighty king whose deeds so far have been unrecorded and unknown. John names the king Dolopathos, that is, one who suffers treachery or grief, and sets the tale at Palermo in Sicily during the reign of Augustus Caesar. The rule of Dolopathos is so beneficent, just, and firm that crime has been eliminated and peace prevails throughout the island. But some subjects plot against Dolopathos, out of envy. They go to Rome and complain to Augustus and the Roman Senate, alleging that Dolopathos has enslaved Sicily and the neighboring territories and that his tyranny not only exalts the wicked and debases the good, but also diminishes the Roman power. Not committing himself, Augustus summons the king to Rome, where he and his adversaries confront each other. Dolopathos counters their repeated accusations and invites Augustus to send an envoy to Sicily to find the truth. The envoy discovers that the subjects of Dolopathos love him like a father but regard his enemies as evil traitors. Augustus punishes the slanderers as they deserve: they are torn apart by wild horses.

viii

Now Augustus and Dolopathos become such good friends that he remits Sicily's tribute forever and also gives Dolopathos his wife's sister, the daughter of Agrippa, in marriage, and bestows other benefits, raising Dolopathos and his kingdom to high status. After many years, the queen becomes pregnant. Dolopathos calls together the wise men and astrologers of the kingdom, who tell him that the child will be a boy; he will become a great philosopher, will suffer much treachery, will rule in Sicily, and will worship the greatest god.

When the boy Lucinius reaches his seventh year, Dolopathos and his advisers consider the best way to educate him and decide to follow the Platonic ideal of the philosopher-king. Dolopathos sends Lucinius to the poet and philosopher Virgil, who is living in Rome. Fearing the treachery mentioned years before by the astrologers, Dolopathos also instructs Virgil to guard the prince well. Virgil finds Lucinius so quick to learn that he easily outstrips all the other pupils and becomes renowned as a master of the arts and philosophy. Thinking it intolerable that such honor should be paid to a mere boy, some men hold a banquet in honor of Lucinius at which they poison his wine. The scheme miscarries. Thanks to his knowledge of astrology, Lucinius exposes them and forces them to drink their own concoction. Though his fame and honor grow, Lucinius remains modest and humble.

One day in the seventh year of his training, while deep in the study of astrology, Lucinius cries out and faints. He is revived with difficulty. When Virgil returns, Lucinius tells him that he has discovered that his mother has died and that his father Dolopathos has remarried and has sent for him to return to Sicily. Unfortunately Virgil, because of some matters in Rome, cannot accompany Lucinius to Sicily, but he asks him to swear a strange oath: not to speak until he and Virgil meet again. The next day, when the youth departs with his father's envoys, the sworn silence begins—and it is maintained, despite the envoys' fears that they will be blamed. In Sicily, after the greetings and sacrifice of thanks to the gods, Lucinius retires to his room, where Dolopathos comes to visit him. In a moving speech, the king tells his son that he is going to abdicate in the youth's favor. When Lucinius still remains silent, Dolopathos is stunned and angry. He blames Virgil and the envoys. The boy explains in writing that no one is guilty.

As news of Lucinius's affliction spreads, the nobles of the court agree that sadness at his mother's death has caused him to become mute, and they prescribe allopathic treatment: to regain his happiness, and thus his speech, he must be enticed to pleasure by all the delights of the flesh. The new queen, his step-mother, volunteers her help and the services of the ladies of the court. Dolopathos promises her half his kingdom if she succeeds. But when her ladies do not make headway in their enterprise, the queen decides to take an active part herself and attempts to seduce the boy. Lucinius is horrified, but he will not speak. She persists, until finally she is caught in her own trap: she falls in love with Lucinius. What follows conforms to the classic pattern of the lustful but rejected stepmother: she accuses Lucinius of trying to rape her.[4] The nobles demand justice and urge death by fire. Though torn by conflicting emotions, Dolopathos finally approves the sentence and himself lights the fire for his son's death. But no one dares throw the boy in.

Suddenly an old man of reverend aspect appears. He is one of the seven sages of Rome, who travels the world teaching and learning. When he hears the charge against Lucinius, he expresses astonishment, asks if he may tell a story, and at the end of the story, asks Dolopathos to postpone the execution for a day and search the laws again.

This scene is repeated every day for seven days. Each day a different sage appears and tells a different story. On the eighth day, however, it is Virgil himself who appears. Now Lucinius is at last able to speak. Virgil tells a final story illustrating the depravity of woman, and then points out that a mute person, unable to speak in his own defense, cannot be legally tried. Lucinius is freed, and the queen and her attendants are burned in his place.

In the same year Dolopathos and Virgil die, and Lucinius then succeeds to his father's throne. After some time a Christian missionary arrives on the island and eventually converts Lucinius. King and missionary go to Jerusalem, where they spend their remaining years.

In *Dolopathos*, the stories have the following order: 1. *Canis* (The Dog); 2. *Gaza* (The Treasure); 3. *Senex* (The Old Man); 4. *Creditor* (The Creditor); 5. *Viduae filius* (The Son of the Widow); 6. *Latronis fillii* (The Sons of the Bandit)—within this last story are contained two other stories: 7. *Polyphemus*, and 8. *Striges* (The Witches); 9. *Cygni* (The Swans); and 10. *Puteus* (The Well). The frame of the stories—the queen's accusation of attempted rape—shows that we are dealing with a series known as the Cycle of the Seven Sages. There are two parts to the Cycle: the eastern part, known as the *Book of Sindebar*, and the western part, known as the *Seven Sages of Rome*. I shall discuss these two parts more fully later.

Johannes de Alta Silva is a conscious literary stylist. Though in his preface he claims to be illiterate, this cannot be taken seriously. His work shows much knowledge of classical literature, history, and philosophy. He has a sense of humor—as evidenced by his attribution to Socrates of worship of the unknown god. He quotes classical authors directly or indirectly over forty times, especially Horace, Vergil, Ovid, Statius, and Lucan, and cites names from philosophy and mythology regularly (see the *Index nominum*). His store of rhetorical devices includes puns, mock epic style, alliteration, assonance, onomatopoeia, and chiasmus. He has two puns upon *Virgilius* and *virga.*[5] Some devices are, of course, difficult to show in translation, especially puns (the numbers refer to pages and lines in Hilka's text):

. . . ceterum autem sine Virgilio suo, cum fidei sue commissus esset et magisterii eius virgam supra modum pertimesceret. . . . (16.10–11)

. . . he did not dare to do anything at all without his teacher Virgil who was his guardian and whose ferule he feared very much. . . .

. . . paremque eum sibi in omni facultate Virgilius predicaret, nunquam tamen ei consedere voluit vel equari, sed semper sub virga eius et disciplina mansit. . . . (18.4–5)

. . . Virgil proclaimed that he was equal to him in every way, nevertheless he never was willing to sit in his presence or be considered his equal. He always remained under his ferule and discipline. . . .

Puns on the meaning of the name Dolopathos are also found often: "non dolor . . . sed dolus" (40.24–25: "not grief . . . but treachery"); "attendite et videte si est dolor sicut dolor meus" (41.25: "consider and see if there is any grief like mine"); and almost immediately after, "Dolopathos . . . assumit dolorem" (41.32: "his great grief increased").

The mock epic style, always used to describe dawn or evening, often contains other stylistic devices:

Cumque iam rutilans aureis aurora radiis ˜uum terris iubar infunderet Luciferque dudum precurrens Phebum Arcton proximum testaretur . . . (23.7–9)

When the dawn gleaming with its golden rays poured its beams upon the earth, and the rising Lucifer bore witness that Phoebus Arctos was approaching . . .

Cum igitur Phebus noctis obscure depulsis tenebris letior solito aureum terris iubar spargens optatum sua presentia crastinum illustrasset. . . . (26.27–29)

When Phoebus, happier than usual, had scattered the shadows of the dark night and, sprinkling his golden rays upon the lands, had illuminated the hoped-for tomorrow with his presence. . . .

Night also arrives in the same mock-epic manner:

Verum cum Phebus suo cursu peracto in Esperias se recepisset undas noxque sopori quietique hominum ordinata previis tenebris advenisset. . . . (30.8–10)

But when Phoebus had run his course and dipped into the western waves; when night, ordained for the sleep and quiet of men, casting its shadows before it, had arrived. . . .

An excellent example of oxymoron occurs when the queen falls madly in love with Lucinius: "Fitque spolium predatrix" (36.24): "the huntress became the prey." The following are examples of chiasmus, alliteration, assonance, and onomatopoeia:

. . . exhibeas te in rege philosophum et in philosopho regem, regiam philosophie disciplina temperans maiestatem commendansque philosophiam regie maiestati. . . . (21.7–9)

. . . show yourself to be a philosopher king and a king philosopher. Temper your kingly majesty with the training of philosophy, and entrust philosophy to the care of your kingly majesty. . . .

Et ecce ipse rex stipatus militum suorum multitudine cum mimorum saltatricumque ac cytharedorum cytharesantium in cytharis suis agmine advenit, sedens super equum dignum regie maiestatis. (27.13–16)

Suddenly the king himself, accompanied by his troops of soldiers and followed by a column of actors, dancers, fluters fluting on their flutes, arrived on a horse worthy of its master.

. . . succede patri forti, tu fortior feliciorque felici, gesta me tuis amplioribus illustrans factis. (32.7–9)

. . . let a stronger man take the throne of his strong father, let a more fortunate man succeed his fortunate father, make my deeds more famous by your greater ones.

. . . assistebant, assidebant. . . . (35.2)

. . . stayed near Lucinius and tended him. . . .

. . . non enim est astucia super astuciam serpentis nec malicia super maliciam mulieris. . . . (35.16–17)

. . . for there is no cunning beyond the cunning of the serpent, nor evil beyond the evil of woman . . . .

Finally, the words of Virgil as he curses the queen are a climax of invective and alliteration:

O, ait, furor, o scelus, o nequicia, o malicia mulieris, o vere monstrum, mulier, monstruosius cunctis monstris, quis tantum scelus vidit, quis audivit, quis huic simile cognovit nec cogitavit? (87.31 *ff.*)

"O madness," he cried, "O wickedness, O baseness, O evil woman, O woman truly a monster more monstrous than all monsters! Who has ever seen or heard such wickedness! Who has ever known or thought anything like this?"

The speech of the sixth wise man is worth noting particularly because John here seems to be trying to adapt his words to his character, which is pompous and pseudophilosophical. This is not the only place where John tries to do this. The attempt is also seen in some of the speeches of the queen, her handmaiden, and King Dolopathos. We thus have an author of the late twelfth or early thirteenth century showing a sense of psychological realism which is remarkable.

Verum ut de instantibus aliquid loquar, uti ex consequentia tuorum pertendere queo verborum, quod tamen sine tui tuorumque iniuria dixerim, nec verum nec verisimile, immo penitus inconsequens michi vicetur filium tuum sompniasse saltem hoc scelus nedum voluisse dicam. (70.19–23)

But to speak about the present, as I can foresee from the logical consequences of your words that I may speak without insulting you or your friends, it seems to me to be neither true nor similar to the truth but rather absolutely illogical to think that your son could even have dreamed of this crime, much less have wished to do it.

There are seven stories in John which are found nowhere else in the Cycles. Of these seven, three (*Creditor, Polyphemus, Cygni*) are of special interest because they have important themes which are found elsewhere in European literature. *Creditor* has as its heroine a woman skilled in the magic arts. When her husband is about to be mutilated because of failure to pay a debt, she disguises herself in men's clothing and, using her legal talent, wins his release. This, of course, is the "pound of flesh" theme and may occur here in written form for the first time in European literature.

Polyphemus may be a parody of the Cyclops story as found in Homer. John may not have read Homer in the original but he could easily have known the story from many other sources. In his story a robber band and its leader are captured by a cannibalistic giant more than thirteen cubits tall, who lives in a dwelling (*habitatio*), and has diseased eyes. When it is time for him to be eaten, the robber pretends to be a doctor who can heal diseased eyes and pours poison into them instead. He eventually escapes by pretending to be one of the giant's rams. Finally, just as in Homer, the giant promises a gift to the robber. In this case, however, the gift turns out to be a magic ring which forces its wearer to keep saying, "Here I am!" The only way he can get rid of the ring is to bite off his finger and throw it away.[6]

In the story of the swans we find for the first time the legend of Lohengrin. This is the common folk tale of humans changed into swans, although the nymph (mother) is not betrayed by any flaw in her conduct. It is the evil mother-in-law who causes the tragedy. This tale contains, as does *Striges*, some striking descriptions of nature.

Many of the other tales show the careful hand of a conscious literary craftsman. In *Senex* the epigrammatic ending is worthy of a Martial, and the description of the little boy as an actor shows traces of true talent. *Viduae filius* takes up only thirty-six lines but is a masterpiece of condensed prose. In ten lines alone John uses six diminutives to create a mock-pathetic atmosphere. *Striges*, which has a forced ending, creates an atmosphere of mock-horror with its description of monsters and cannibalism.

Some of the other tales seem to end too quickly. In *Canis*, the one story common to all three versions of the Cycle, John has omitted (or has not heard of) the tournament and the nurses. He has, however, given two other possessions to the father, a horse and a hawk. They, as well as the dog, are all killed in a fit of rage. *Gaza*, as noted above, is much shorter than the later version by Herbert and ends so abruptly that it almost seems as if John tired of the story.[7]

But these are minor defects. The work, judged as a whole, contains much that is of interest and should receive its fair place in European literature. There is always the possibility that other analogues, earlier than John's tales, may still be discovered.

The Book of Sindebar

The eastern versions of the tale of the lustful wife, known as the *Book of Sindebar*, appear to have no direct written connection with the western versions, known as *The Seven Sages of Rome*, although they have many features in common. The former takes its title from the name of the teacher of the young prince—Sindebar (Sindbād, Sindibad). This is the general outline of the plot:

A certain king summons seven wise men and gives them his son to be educated. The sage Sindebar convinces the king that he is the best teacher and so is able to obtain control of the boy's training. In many cases the boy does not learn easily, but Sindebar's skill overcomes all obstacles. One of the interesting methods of Sindebar's teaching is that he builds a temple, which has the learning of the ages painted on the walls and ceiling, where the boy lives. In six months (the times varies), when it is time for the boy's return, his horoscope is cast, and it is learned that if he speaks before a certain time he will die. On his return he remains mute, the king is enraged, and the young queen (or concubine) attempts to cure him. The accusation of attempted rape follows. The boy is condemned and the sentence of death is passed. The king's wise men, however, attempt to save the boy, each one telling two stories each day for seven days. The stories are countered by one story of the queen's. Finally, when the boy can speak, he accuses the queen and tells a story (or stories), and the queen is condemned.

Clouston has noted that this frame story has many resemblances to a Hindu collection in Sanskrit.

The repeated failures to educate the prince, the father's grief and rage, and the sage finally undertaking to instruct the youth in *six months* correspond exactly with the frame of the *Pancha Tantra (Five Chapters)*, a celebrated collection of Hindu fables in Sanskrit, as old at least as the sixth century, and the resemblance can hardly be merely fortuitous.[8]

This sounds reasonable, but possibly somewhat strongly worded. There are so many aspects of these versions which seem fortuitous that it is dangerous to be too positive about relationships and resemblances. The excellent work of Clouston, however, cannot be denied. He also pointed out, referring to Benfey's work,[9] that the frame of the *Book of Sindebar* is the same as a story about Asoka (Açoka, d. 232 B.C.), the great Indian king and Buddhist, as well as that found in many other forms in Indian literature.

The source of the *Book of Sindebar* is unknown. All authorities agree that the first version was created somewhere east of Europe. The usually accepted view is that it originated in India and spread from east to west. If this is the case, it probably begins in Sanskrit, then proceeds to Persia where it is translated into Pahlavi and from Pahlavi is translated into Arabic by one Musa (Moūsos) about the eighth century A.D.[10] This work, like the previous ones, is lost, but it very likely is the version on which all others are based.[11]

From the Arabic there are now extant a Syriac version (tenth-eleventh centuries A.D.) from which a Greek version arose (eleventh century A.D.); an old Spanish version (1253); and a Hebrew version, date unknown, from which a Latin version was made (c. 1400). There are, of course, other versions of this work. The most clear and concise descriptions of them can be found in Campbell's introduction. A complete outline of the probable genealogy is found in Professor Runte's *Li Ystoire de la male marastre, Version M of the Roman des sept sages de Rome*, p. xiv, which I present here. It is uncertain where John's work fits in.[12]

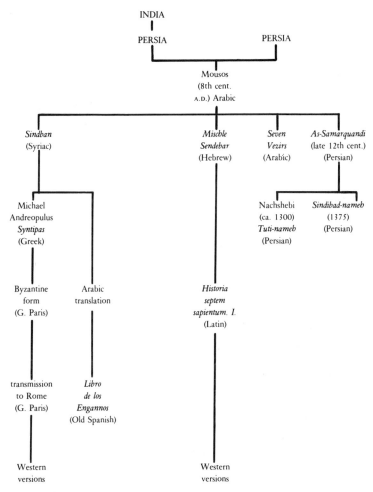

INDIA

PERSIA   PERSIA

Mousos
(8th cent.
A.D.) Arabic

Sindban
(Syriac)

Mischle
Sendebar
(Hebrew)

Seven
Vezirs
(Arabic)

As-Samarquandi
(late 12th cent.)
(Persian)

Michael
Andreopulus
Syntipas
(Greek)

Nachshebi
(ca. 1300)
Tuti-nameh
(Persian)

Sindibad-nameh
(1375)
(Persian)

Byzantine
form
(G. Paris)

Arabic
translation

Historia
septem
sapientum. I.
(Latin)

transmission
to Rome
(G. Paris)

*Libro
de los
Engannos*
(Old Spanish)

Western
versions

Western
versions

Naturally, other theories about the origin and transmission of these tales exist. Morris Epstein believes that the original language was Hebrew.[13] Ben Edwin Perry has hypothesized that the influence went not from east to west, but from west to east, and that the original language was Pahlavi.[14] A recent article by George Artola, however, attempts to rejuvenate the Indian origin.[15] Of the many theories which have evolved Perry's has probably been the most influential in recent years. No doubt there will be re-examination of these theories. When we consider, however, that nothing is definitely known before the time of Musa (eighth century A.D.), and that even the author's name and his work are doubtful, then we must move slowly. Professor Runte puts it aptly when he says, "From a lost Persian *mythographos* the Arab Mousos composed in the eighth century a work which is also lost. . . ."[16] When so much is left to conjecture and little or nothing left to fact, then nothing can be positive. Unless some facts or new evidence can be discovered one should accept these theories with an open mind and be reluctant to adopt any one to the exclusion of others.

The Seven Sages of Rome

Just how *The Seven Sages* as it appeared in the East in the *Book of Sindibād* became the story as it flourished in Western Europe is a question not easy to answer. The problem is rendered a most difficult one by the circumstance that the parent Western version has been lost. Indeed, our only knowledge of it is such as is wholly inferential in nature.[17]

A familiar situation. The questions are the same in the west as in the east. Where or what did it come from? How did it get west? And who brought it? It is generally assumed that *The Seven Sages*, as found in the west, developed from the versions of the east. This is not only because of the framework about the wicked stepmother, but also because there are some of the same stories in both traditions.

It might be possible that the story of the lustful wife, or the wicked step-mother, could develop independently, as a universal concept illustrating the depravity of woman. We have seen this theme in the Egyptian tales of Anapou and Satou, and in Joseph in Egypt, and in Homer, none of which seems to have a connection or relationship with the other, and there are many other cultures where this idea has developed, However, when there are four similar stories (*canis, aper, senescalus,* and *avis*) told by wise men in both traditions, then we must assume that there is a relationship between the eastern and the western versions. Whether the relationship is primarily oral or written may never be known. Certainly an oral tradition (as in the case of Homer) precedes a written tradition. We may assume that the eastern tradition originally was an oral one. It does not necessarily follow, however, that the first person to bring these tales to the west heard them. He might easily have seen a manuscript. Campbell, however, believes that the many differences between the two versions "demonstrate beyond any reasonable doubt that the Western parent version grew out of oral account."[18]

There are several conjectures as to what the source of the original western version was. The most probable one, and the one which most scholars accept, is the Greek *Syntipas*, which the prologue states was written by Michael Andreopulus. Its date is uncertain (1050–1100?) but Paris has assumed that it came to Europe through the Byzantine Empire in various stages and revisions to Italy, *or* possibly through Arabia, *or* possibly it was brought by the Jews to Spain.[19] There weren't many other ways to get to Europe.

Another attractive theory is that the original source of the western group was the Hebrew version, which shows some similarities to *The Seven Sages of Rome*.[20] In the Hebrew, as in the western versions, the sages are named; they all want to instruct the prince; they, not the counselors, defend the prince; in *aper* the adventure happens to a man, not an ape; in *avis* the bird is deceived through an opening in the roof and the maid acts as an accomplice to the wife. But, as Campbell points out,[21] these similarities might be of no consequence, and some might come about naturally.

The idea of the Hebraic origin and influence of *Mischle Sendabar* has been given new impetus by the work of Morris Epstein. He suggests that the *Book of Sindibād*, as we have it, may be Hebraic in origin;[22] that it "may have appeared in Pahlavi in the sixth or seventh century of our era. . . . cloaked in Arab garb it made its way from one spellbound audience to another until it reached the west." He suggests that the disseminators of the work may have been the Radanites, the roving Jewish merchantmen who traveled all over the world.

This theory, tentatively proposed as it is, deserves serious consideration and is as likely as any of the others. No direct proof has been discovered, nor do the other ideas offer any convincing evidence. All that is known is that there exist (or existed) eastern versions from which the western versions probably sprang (see Runte's table, p. xv above). How the eastern version originally came to the west is also unknown. Campbell and others suggest that a Crusader may have been the agent of transmission, to whom "its Buddhistic flavor may be imagined to have made a strong appeal. The time of transmission cannot have been later than the middle of the twelfth century, which . . . must be made the superior limit for the dating of the first Western version."[23]

The date which is mentioned here is probably accurate, since it was shown that *Dolopathos* probably was written late in the twelfth century, and its author, Johannes de Alta Silva, tells us that he has written about things which he heard. The idea of the Crusader returning home carrying the *Book of Sindibād* with him is intriguing and glamorous, but it is too narrow a point of view. Long before the Crusades, men made pilgrimages to the Holy Land. In every century of recorded Christian history, pilgrimages are known to have occurred. In the eleventh century alone, before the First Crusade, one hundred and seventeen were recorded, and one, made by the Bishop of Bamberg, included eleven thousand followers.[24] To confine the transmission of the *Book of Sindibād* to a solitary Crusader is to ignore the possibility that long before the Crusades one or more people may have returned to Europe bringing back one or more of the eastern versions. Nor must it be assumed that the versions of which we now have knowledge were the only ones in existence. The framework lends itself to almost any kind of story. It is possible that many of the stories which are found in the west and which are no longer found in the east originally came from the east, but the sources have disappeared.

The arrangement of these stories again contributes nothing to our understanding of the other groups. Here it can be seen how completely *Dolopathos* is outside both traditions. It contains only one story (*canis*) which is also found in the *Book of Sindibād*, and only three stories (*canis, gaza,* and *puteus*) found in *The Seven Sages of Rome*. *Canis*, then, is the only story found in all three versions. We have no record where the other stories came from or how John came upon the teller of the tales. The fact that John says he heard the stories may or may not imply an oral tradition. If we tell a person a story written by Hans Christian Anderson, the person will say that he heard the story, but there is no oral tradition involved. Campbell certainly goes too far when he states: "Such far-reaching changes establish conclusively that the parent Western version was not a translation from any Eastern version. . . . They seem to me to make it extremely probable that this author had no sort of first-hand acquaintance with any of the Eastern versions."[25]

This statement should probably be qualified somewhat. The extant eastern versions show a great difference from those of the west. But how many versions have perished? Of the thousands of pilgrims who traveled to the Holy Land before and after the First Crusade, how many heard or read hundreds of tales which no longer exist; and how many brought them back to the west? We shall never know. Amid such a cloud of uncertainties it is best to avoid such positive statements as "establish conclusively" and "extremely probable."

Notes to Introduction

1. Gaston Paris, *La Littérature française au moyen âge*, 3rd edition (Paris: Hachette, 1905), p. 109, dated it around the end of the twelfth century. H. Oesterley, *Dolopathos sive de Rege et Septem Sapientibus* (Strassburg, 1873), p. xi, dated it around 1184–85. The text used for this translation and for citations in the introduction is the edition by Alfons Hilka, *Historia Septem Sapientum II. Johannis de Alta Silva Dolopathos sive de Rege et Septem Sapientibus* (Heidelberg, 1913). The numbers of the Latin text refer to page and line.

2. In *Romania* 2 (1873): 497, in a review of Oesteley's edition of *Dolopathos*, Paris dated the Old French poem before 1223. Charles Brunet and Anatole de Montaiglon, *Li Romans di Dolopathos* (Paris, 1856), p. xix, dated it between 1223 and 1226.

3. Herbert's version of "Gaza" is longer and his last story is completely different — it is "Inclusa," not found in John and summed up by Killis Campbell, *The Seven Sages of Rome* (Boston, 1907), pp. cix–cxii.

4. Stories about the lustful stepmother (or the lustful wife) who accuses someone of attempted rape are numerous. The earliest extant version is the Egyptian story of "The Two Brothers," Anapou and Satou, which has been ably summarized by William A. Clouston, *The Book of Sindibad; or, The Story of the King, his Son, the Damsel, and the Seven Vazirs. From the Persian and Arabic, with Introduction, Notes, and Appendix* (Glasgow: Cameron, 1884), pp. xxiv–xxvi. Clouston accepts the date "from the fourteenth century B.C.," p. xxiii. Compare also Joseph P. Yohannan, *Joseph and Poitiphar's Wife in World Literature*, (New York: New Directions, 1968), pp. 10–13. Here the brothers are called Anpu and Bata. In addition to Potiphar's wife we have Bellerophon in Book 6 of the *Iliad*; also the story of Hippolytus and Phaedra.

5. The Latin word *virga* I have translated as "ferule." It also means a

(magician's) wand. In the Middle Ages Vergil was considered to have magical or divine powers; thus the spelling of the name Virgil used in the tale.

6. Compare Sir James Frazer, *Apollodorus, The Library*, 2 vols. (Cambridge: Harvard University Press, 1954). In the appendix, Frazer concludes that this tale follows not the Homeric account but an oral tradition (pp. 404–55).

7. This is the story of Rhampsinitis found in Herodotus, *History* 2. 121. It is extremely popular and has been found in China and Japan. Compare Hideichi Matsubara, "Chinese and Japanese Versions of *Gaza*," in *Studies on the Seven Sages of Rome and Other Medieval Essays*, ed. by H. Niedzielski, H. R. Runte, W. L. Hendrickson (Honolulu: Educational Research Associates, 1978), pp. 104–7.

8. Clouston, p. xxi.

9. Clouston, p. xxix. Theodor Benfey, *Pantschatantra* (Leipzig, 1899). See also Hans R. Runte, *Li Ystoire de la male marastre, Version M of the Roman des sept sages de Rome* (Tübingen: Max Niemeyer Verlag, 1974), p. xii.

10. Compare Runte, pp. xii–xiii.

11. Compare Campbell, p. xi.

12. Campbell thinks it likely that John was acquainted with a version of *The Seven Sages of Rome*, p. xx.

13. Morris Epstein, *Tales of Sendabar* (Philadelphia, 1967).

14. Ben Edwin Perry, "Origins of the Book of Sindbād ," *Fabula* 3 (Berlin: 1959–60), pp. 1–94.

15. George Artola, "The Nature of the Book of Sindbād ," in *Studies on the Seven Sages of Rome*, ed. H. Niedzielski, H. R. Runte, W. L. Hendrickson, pp. 7–31.

16. Runte, p. xii.

17. Campbell, p. xv.

18. Campbell, p. xvi.

19. Gaston Paris, *La Littérature française au moyen âge*, 3rd edition (Paris: Hachette, 1905).

20. I rely here upon the discussion of Campbell, pp. xvi–xvii.

21. Campbell, p. xvii.

22. Morris Epstein, "Mishle Sendebar: New Light on the Transmission of Folklore from East to West," *American Academy for Jewish Research Proceedings*, 1958, pp. 2–17.

23. Campbell, p. xvii.

24. Sydney M. Brown, *Medieval Europe* (New York: Harcourt Brace & Co., 1932), p. 242.

25. Earlier I tended to agree with this view. Compare Gilleland, "The *Dolopathos* of Johannes de Alta Silva: A New Evaluation," in *Studies on the Seven Sages of Rome*, p. 37.

Dolopathos

Dedication

TO OUR REVEREND FATHER and lord Bertrand, bishop of Metz by the grace of God, greetings. Brother Johannes, one of the monks of Alta Silva, hopes that he will live long and happily and end the course of his life in peace.

For a long time I used to seek amid the quiet of the cloisters and the robes of the priests a man who would please my heart. I mean a man virtuous, holy, just, and perfect, one learned in divine as well as human laws. I sought, I failed to find, and finally I lost hope. I regretted that I had wasted my time and that in all the churches of Christ known to me no such man existed. There was no one who could properly and worthily perform the duties of pastor or even hireling, as I thought.[1] This affected me so much that my eyes would fill with tears, and I would weep continually.

At long last, however, my sorrow was removed by the splendor of your holiness, brighter than light. My joy was all the greater because of the length and difficulty of my search. Your Holiness seemed to me so much more wonderful and excellent because in these evil days a man like you is a rare and difficult discovery. These are the times when the son of man can scarcely find a place to lay his head,[2] as the Scripture tells us. There are no longer saints or prophets. And as the people act, so do the priests. An axe of gold is a rare tool and "as rare on the earth as a black swan."[3]

But we must not wonder that virtue becomes more precious because of its rarity, although philosophers tell us that it cannot be diminished or increased. If everything becomes more valuable in proportion to its scarcity, a man of virtue and knowledge must be considered precious beyond price. Among millions of men throughout the whole world, he can be found only with difficulty. Your holiness, a strong light blazing in a dark place,[4] has impelled me to send to Your Excellency the first fruits of what little talent I have, a small work called *The King and the Seven Wise Men*. I do this not because I believe that your light will shine stronger because of me, but that I may become brighter and better because of you. I hope that your wise suggestions will improve it and that it will receive the support of your patronage. Please deem it worthwhile to receive this little book dedicated to you, the first fruit of the tree which your friend, my lord Henry, venerable steward of my monastery, has planted. Pray treat this little book kindly and do not judge it harshly, so that if I ever write anything more I may respectfully come to you again.

There is only one thing which I earnestly ask. Please deem it worthwhile to write back to me some remarks about this book so that your letter may be placed in the work and give it support and patronage. A fond farewell, most holy father.

Preface

ALL THE EFFORTS of the ancient philosophers were spent in seeking the true nature of things by careful inquiry. They described without embellishment the wars of kings and the deeds of famous men exactly as they occurred, and left a record of true history to instruct and delight posterity. Because of their great effort they attained such heights that they deserve to be praised as if they were more than mortal and revered like gods with statues and divine honors.

Some contemporary writers yearn for the fame of the ancients, but they are unable to imitate the style, and their works are filled with lies. They prefer to write about unearned glory or the faults of men rather than to tell the truth for all to see. Some have even tried to corrupt the pure and simple truth with lies and covered lies with the cloak of truth. This they have done of their own free will, impelled by prejudice and unreason. They have praised to the stars some men who were unworthy and undeserving, and exalted them over others with improper adulation. Some better men, however, they have attacked like mad dogs, chewing them to bits. There is neither rhyme nor reason in their praise or blame. They have never heard of Horace's wonderful "golden mean"⁵ but have slipped into the opposite fault and gone too far to the right or the left. Dirty and foul, like snakes and serpents, they creep along the ground, or rather like unclean pigs they enjoy swamps and filth. Or they go to the opposite extreme and puff themselves up with wind instead of knowledge. They become bladders and roar out windy words, and like straw or a summer cloud caught by the breeze they are carried through the empty air until they vanish completely.

There have been some men who play at philosophizing, or possibly I should say ranting, who write things which could not possibly have happened. The fools fill up their books with ghosts and monstrosities and try to join opposites together. When they have stuffed their books with these things they expect men to read their nonsense. Nevertheless, there is one good thing which writers of this type do. When they mention the different laws and justice of countries and cities, when they describe the customs and deeds of bad men as well as good, when they try to relieve human suffering with their jesting, they force their future readers to become critics and judge the good from the bad.

Once when I was deep in the study and admiration of the classics, I happened to recall the history of a certain king and the amazing things which happened to him during his reign. No writer had yet written about him, possibly because no one else had heard of his deeds, and I was worried lest the great history of this great king pass into oblivion as time went by. Although I am rather stupid and have no talent or training, I decided nevertheless to write about these things as best I could. I did not want to color (or rather discolor) the subject with an ornamental display of words but rather to write the history just as it happened in a simple prose style. If, however, I have attempted something beyond my strength, please do not consider me rash or presumptuous. I have undertaken this task not for vain and useless glory but as an exercise in style, and because I love history. Now, reader, if you find anything crude or unsuitable, please pardon me. Remember, I have not sweated long over the rules of Priscian, nor have I reclined in the flowery gardens of Quintilian and Cicero. But so much for all this. Kindly open the gate and walk in.

Dolopathos

OR

The King

and the Seven Wise Men

W HEN THE DIVINE AUGUSTUS was ruling the Romans he was not content with the borders of Italy but extended his power throughout the four corners of the earth. He governed all the kings and nobles under his dominion with justice and mercy. There was at this time a certain king of Trojan descent who, as if by some deadly foreknowledge of future events, was named Dolopathos, a name composed from the Greek and Latin tongues which means "one who suffers treachery or grief."

After the death of his father under the law of Augustus Caesar he inherited the rich kingdom of Sicily, although he was still a boy, and administered its affairs properly and vigorously. He always considered the advice of the wise men and elders of the kingdom, and with their assistance he crushed rebellion when it began and handled civil cases at home. As he grew older his strength, virtue, and wisdom increased. He became a handsome young man, and his excellent qualities developed even further as time went by. Everywhere people spoke of his uprightness.

He inspired such respect in great kingdoms, near and far, that the kings, who were concerned for their thrones, bought his friendship with precious gifts. Each one realized that he could not remain in power if he offended King Dolopathos in any way at all. Nor was this amazing, for he was most energetic in waging war, most generous in bestowing gifts, and most eloquent in speech. Some he overcame with weapons, some with gifts, and some with sweet words. He treated the weak and the conquered so gently and kindly that you would think he was a father, not a king, and that they were his sons, not his slaves. He defended the cause of widows and orphans, and by his gifts he relieved the poverty of the poor, thinking that injustice to them reflected upon himself. The unjust man was punished as quickly and severely as possible. He was particularly compassionate towards little children, but against the proud and the wicked he raged in such a way you would think he was acting like a wild animal, more like a tiger than a man.

If a man was caught in crime, neither gold, nor silver, nor friends, nor noble birth protected him; even if he were of kingly blood he received punishment worthy of his deeds. It was unsafe for bandits and criminals to live even in deserted places. No cave, no cliff protected them, and just as the dove is always on guard against the destructive hawk, so they kept watch for the king even when he was in the farthest parts of his kingdom. Banditry disappeared, crimes languished, and all the wicked, who formerly were accustomed to live by robbing the poor, turned to better things and even joyfully aided the poor with their own money. Each criminal had to choose one of three things which he could not avoid: to change his evil habits to better ones; to leave his king and country like a wild beast; or to die.

Thus the farmer happily tilled his fields, and the traveler safely went his way. There was no longer need for locks and bars, since throughout the extent of the kingdom there was no robber. Fleecy sheep and other types of animals grazed on the mountain tops, and fruit grew abundantly in the valleys.[6] Trees of every kind were burdened with their fruit, and the vines with difficulty sustained the grapes. The granaries were filled with grain, the presses dripped wine and oil,[7] the land flowed with milk and honey,[8] and the homes of all were rich in silver and gold and an abundance of all things. Even the elements themselves, as if somehow obeying the wish of the king, so tempered the changes of the seasons that in winter or summer it seemed always to be spring.

Because of this good fortune the people enjoyed continual good health, long life, and many children. Why go on? But their affluent life brought pride and luxury. Since the weapons of Mars were unused, the arrows of Cupid and the camp of Venus weakened their manly spirits. No longer did they seek glory in arms, because all turned their thoughts to pleasure, and the flesh, and the embraces of women. The young man sported with the young girl, the child played with the child, the old man and the old woman chatted together and thought of the past while they drank the pure wine and struggled to see who first could drain the cup.

Although King Dolopathos enjoyed perpetual peace and abundant wealth and held the nations around him in sway, he realized that the spirit of his warriors was becoming slack from the benefits of peace and the enticements of pleasure, and that their manly strength was turning into womanly softness. To cure this disease, he established different types of training for his soldiers: long marches, stone throwing, horse racing, and spear throwing. And he gave fine gifts to those who excelled in the contests. Next, in all the cities of his kingdom, he appointed twelve older men to act as senators to consider civil cases for the good of the city and the kingdom and to govern the subject people justly. He also promoted the sons of retired soldiers to military offices, and he gave honors to each of them according to the worth of his family or the merit of his life. Desiring to exalt his kingdom with even greater glory and piety he began to build in the different cities temples to the gods at great expense and placed priests in them to offer sacrifices every day and to pray for his safety and the stability of the kingdom. The king was indeed a zealous worshipper of the gods, showing extreme piety toward them. This was impiety toward God, but in those lands nothing had as yet been announced about the highest and the true God because the truth, the holiness, which was going to teach men to worship one God in the spirit had not yet descended from the heavens to the earth. Thus people of all ages, men and women, youths and maidens, young and old gave thanks to their gracious king who had given them so much, and sacrificed and prayed to the gods to give him long life and health. During this time the divine Augustus, who magnificently and successfully governed the monarchy of the whole world, often heard about the outstanding integrity of King Dolopathos. Envy was beneath him and he was greatly delighted to hear of his virtues. But since a virtuous man who lives piously will incur jealousy, certain deadly betrayers of their country, who hated peace and quiet and envied men's good fortune, disparaged the deeds of the king. Goaded by hatred of him, steeped in the poison of that one who first destroyed Adam, equal to one another in baseness, colleagues in wickedness, partners in betrayal, speaking with one mind, one desire, one mouth, they developed a plan. They intrigued against the king, they plotted how to get him in a trap and kill him, so that when he was dead they could slander him freely. But they realized that this violence could not be done without danger to themselves. Turning to other plans, therefore, and plotting other things, they sought by what trick or cunning plan they could bring about the wickedest of crimes, and they found nothing safer than to effect by poisonous slander what they did not dare to do openly with a weapon. They sharpened their tongues into swords, they stretched the bow, they put arrows into the quiver to shoot secretly and kill the innocent. Without restraining their baseness longer, when the opportune time arose, they went to the Senate House where, before Caesar and the holy Senate, they vomited forth venom with their triple forked tongues.[9]

But lest their lies be discovered by the wisdom of such men they cunningly smeared honey over the trickery and bitterness of their mind, pretending that their lying words were spoken out of duty, saying that they were the type of men who wished to consider the safety of their fatherland and to protect the republic, and that therefore at great danger they had undertaken such a laborious journey. At first they spoke of their fictitious duty and wheedled like the scorpion, so that later they might securely and carefully sting with the tail.

Caesar, the consuls, the senators, and the Roman nobles were in session when they were ordered to tell the reason why they came, and a great silence fell upon the assembly. Then these foul betrayers broke the silence: "Since the orb of the world obeys your command, O Caesar, and yours, O reverend fathers, it is your duty to provide for the peace and good of rich as well as poor. Since the tyrannies of kings are corrected by the scepter of your justice, and we believe that nothing escapes Your Majesty, although it happens secretly and far away, we wonder whether there has ever come to your merciful ears rumors of the desolation of the kingdom of Sicily. Have you heard of the cruelty of its king and the devastation of the surrounding countryside? For now King Dolopathos, to whom you gave the kingdom of Sicily when still a schoolboy, forgetful of such kindness and ignoring the decrees of Augustus, the consuls, the senators, and the laws of the Romans, rages with strange and unheard-of tyranny against his subjects and the neighboring regions. He captures kings, demanding tribute from them. Those resisting he attacks with constant wars. The nobles of his kingdom he strips of their paternal honors and brings in the ignoble and the wicked. Those condemned to death he pardons and says they are worthy to live. To them he shows favor, but the innocent he destroys with tortures of every kind, especially those who favor the Roman Empire. But why say more? Sicily, richer in gold and silver and every resource than all other kingdoms, is not enough for this king's desires, nor are the lands he has invaded and taken from the Roman rule enough; but rather this arrogant planner of sedition is already revolting from your rule. He has gathered together countless weapons and soldiers with which he conspires against the state. So we, fearful lest the whole country perish on account of the arrogance of one man when this became known to Your Majesty, and considering what was best for ourselves and the state, thought it necessary to bring our grievances to your notice, even if we perished. It is to your interest that he be called to account for such crimes. Therefore, O Caesar, act quickly and do not postpone consideration of such evil, lest delay bring harm to you and the state."

Overcome the evil seeds of sudden disease when they are new.[10]

Resist beginnings; too late is the medicine prepared when the disease has gained strength by long delay.[11]

Although Caesar was a man of subtle character, he was not quite sure whether these words were inspired by hatred and envy or the truth. So on the advice of the senators he spoke to them kindly, ordered them to remain in the city, and implied that they might ex-

pect from him rewards worthy of their faith. They thought that their
evil machinations had turned out as planned and eagerly awaited the
promises of Caesar. Meanwhile Caesar, wishing to know more fully
the truth, sent a curt letter to the king and ordered him to come to
the Senate House to answer certain accusations before him and the
Senate.

After King Dolopathos had read the letter, he summoned all the
elders and nobles of his kingdom and asked whether he should obey
the orders of Caesar or not. They all agreed that it was not safe to
despise the commands of such a prince and that he should be given no
cause for offense, especially since he had not harmed Caesar or plotted against the state. He agreed with the advice of his nobles and
made ready for the journey. Then, accompanied by his friends and
the greatest men in the kingdom, he presented himself as quickly as
possible before Caesar and promised that he would reply to all
charges according to the law of the Senate.

A day was set by Caesar when the king and his opponents would
be heard. At the appointed day the consuls were called, the Senate
and the Roman nobility were summoned. When both sides were present, Caesar gave permission to accuse and to answer accusations.
Those who had made up the lies repeated what they had said before,
but rather timidly, and they added other new lies. King Dolopathos
stood silent for a while and looked around here and there as if
amazed at something strange. At last he began to speak in this way:
"O Caesar, ten years have passed since I received by your kindness
the kingdom of Sicily. It is amazing that in such a length of time not
one of the kings, not one of those against whom my accusers say I
waged war and burdened with tribute has brought a complaint before
Your Majesty. But they enjoy the same freedom as I; they as well as I
have the same defender—you. It is not likely that I would have imposed tribute upon kings against your will, since they, as well as I, are
forced to pay tribute to you every year. But if I had even tried it at
any time, they would have defended themselves and their property
bravely, especially since they are under your protection and authority. Since this charge cannot stand, it follows that my accusers must
have lied in other things. All Sicily and the neighboring kingdoms
know that these men have always been the bloody betrayers of their

country, and I would have considered it unworthy of me to have replied to them even this much had it not been for my respect for you and this assembly. To be sure that these men are as I say and that I have not done what they accuse me of, send an intelligent man, whom you trust, to find out the truth about me and about them from the people of Sicily."

This plan was agreeable to Caesar and the nobles of the Roman Senate. An ambassador was sent who carefully asked many people, in public and in private, what sort of a king he was, what sort were his accusers, and what rumors had been heard about each. Everybody, without exception, noble and common, rich and poor, grieving as if they had already lost their king, with one voice tearfully shouted that they considered Dolopathos a father, not a king but a guardian, not a master but the savior of the country and the defender of the state. They swore that his accusers were betrayers of the country and spillers of human blood who had stained their whole lives with crimes of every description.

When the ambassador returned, he informed Caesar and the Senate of everything he had heard about the king and his enemies. The traitors were summoned, and Caesar said: "Since I promised you rewards worthy of your faith, I think now that I have found a way of justly repaying you as you deserve. So, according to the laws of the Romans and the decrees of the senators and consuls, I order you to be tied to wild horses by your feet and dragged through all the streets and districts of the city as an example and terror to all, while a herald proclaims that the bloody slanderers of their masters deserve such things from the judges of the Roman Senate."

So these men, unworthy to live, died justly. Their bodies were given to the birds of the sky and the beasts of the field, and their souls to the minions of Pluto. Then King Dolopathos and Caesar became such good friends that by a decree of the Senate the tribute of Sicily was revoked forever. Caesar also gave him the sister of his wife, the daughter of Agrippa, in marriage, along with the tributes of the countries and provinces near Sicily, on the condition that King Dolopathos should always protect the Senate and the state with his arms and advice. A little later, with the consent of Caesar, he and his wife happily returned to Sicily.

On his arrival the country, which had mourned his absence, was overjoyed. Everyone was happy and gay because of the victory and glory of their king and they spent the time feasting with games and music. All hailed the king and the queen, wishing them a long and happy reign. Dolopathos summoned the kings and nobles of the provinces and delivered to them the orders of Caesar to pay tribute to him. Without any hesitation they promised faith and homage to him, as Caesar had ordered, and they said that they would serve him loyally in every way, as if he were Caesar.

Then King Dolopathos, exulting in his glory and wealth and wishing his name to endure, built a palace of amazing construction and unbelievable size in a certain city of his kingdom. It was surrounded by shrubbery, meadows, sweet waters, and rich fields, and it has lasted even to the present day. It is called Palermo. In this palace, to pass over many other incredible things, there were as many doors as there are days in the year. In this palace, as big as a city, the king placed the seat of his government, conducted the more holy festivals, and handled the more important cases and businesses.

Nevertheless, although he surpassed all other kings in the abundance of goods which could be brought on land or sea and there was nothing which his glory lacked, there was one thing which lessened his happiness: he had no children, for the queen had not conceived. This was a daily cause of concern, for he feared that after his death the kingdom and his treasures might fall into the hands of strangers. Daily he prayed to the gods and offered sacrifices. He honored them with offerings and tearfully asked them at least to grant him a successor from the queen. After the cycle of many years, when the king had completely given up hope of offspring, the queen conceived and arrived at the time of birth. This happened not because of the kindness or virtue of his gods, since they are nothing, but because of the goodness of the only living and true God.

While she was giving birth, the king summoned the priests and the astrologers to find out from them what fate lay in store for the child who was being born. After they had studied their charts and considered the motion of the stars, they said that the child was a male, that he would live and become a great philosopher and would suffer many injuries. He would rule in the house of his father and become a worshipper of the greatest God. Although these things would happen, they did not learn them from their knowledge of astrology. Rather, He who once gave speech to the ass and induced the prophet Balaam to bless the people of Israel disclosed the secrets of the future and the fate predestined for the son of the king.[12]

Meanwhile the son of the king was born and was named Lucinius. This name comes from the word for light, and he was so named because at his birth a clear light, a bright day of happiness gleamed in the mind of his father. It was ordered that throughout his dominions the day of the birth was to be joyfully celebrated every year. The boy was entrusted to the care of nurses and was brought up very carefully by them for seven years, the usual time set by the ancients for the sons of nobles. Indeed, among the kings and nobles in those days it was the custom not to permit their sons to eat with them during infancy, which ended in the seventh year.

From now on Dolopathos spent the rest of his life happily, since everything had turned out as he wished and his succession was secure. His only care was the rearing of Lucinius. The boy was weaned, and after the cycle of the year had revolved seven times he was no longer considered an undisciplined infant. On his birthday the nurses presented him to his father, who was then by chance conducting a religious banquet for the kings and nobles gathered there. The father was delighted at the sight of his son, and the guests rejoiced with the father. They were amazed at the beauty of the boy, the grace of his limbs, the candor and elegance of his features. In him they reverently saw the image of his father. While they were dining, they spoke about the boy and discussed how he should be educated and what teachers he should have. The king remembered a certain saying of Plato's that the state would be fortunate if philosophers ruled it, or if kings were philosophers.[13] Because of this saying it seemed best to the king and the others that he should be entrusted to a philosopher to be educated in the liberal arts. Guided by the examples of wise men and the recorded deeds of kings and nobles, he would be able to rule himself and his subjects more easily and anticipate the traps of his enemies.

At this time there lived at Rome the very famous poet Virgil, who was well known to the king because he had been born at Mantua, a

city of Sicily, and had often been honored by him. Because he was
known to him and because he was considered the outstanding
philosopher of his time, the father sent his son to him with many gifts
and asked him by the gods to impart his own knowledge to the boy
and to guard him carefully from the traps of the wicked. The king
had learned through the priests and astrologers that the boy would be
exposed to some harm. Because of his reverence and friendship for
the king, Virgil accepted the boy. First he taught him the alphabet
and then, with gentleness and persuasion (as teachers do), in no time
at all he taught him to form a syllable from letters and from syllables
to form a word and from words to construct a sentence. And so,
gradually advancing, the boy began by himself to read and speak both
the Greek and Latin languages. Virgil was very pleased. He was
amazed at the speed and natural ability of the boy, and when he
realized that he showed great promise he paid more attention to him.
The boy, whose talent was outstanding, listened carefully to his
teacher and whatever he heard once and understood he never forgot
because of his innate genius. There was no need to ask his teacher a
second time about it. So it happened that within the course of a year
he surpassed those who were older and had been studying with
teachers for five or even seven years, and he asked Virgil to instruct
him in even more advanced things. When Virgil realized that the
child had advanced so rapidly that he was ready to begin training in
the arts, he gladly acceded to his wish. Because Virgil loved the liberal
arts so much he had turned his amazing genius to the composition of
a small handbook which enabled one to learn those vast subjects in a
short time. In three years anyone could learn perfectly what he
himself had been able to learn only with great labor. He was unwilling to let anyone, teacher or pupil, see this book even for an
hour—not even Augustus, the ruler of the world. But he gave it to
Lucinius, for whom he had written it, because he wished him to pro-
gress rapidly. In his room, apart from others, they would discuss the
liberal arts like two friends.

First he taught him grammar, the mother of the arts, which
Lucinius grasped with such speed that even Virgil was
astonished. Then they came to dialectic, and it is amazing to say how
shrewd he was. Not even trained teachers were more ingenious in

proposing questions or quicker in solving them than he. From there he advanced to the flowery fields of rhetoric where he attained complete mastery of the charm of eloquence. When these three subjects had been fully mastered he turned to the other four, which we call the quadrivium, and learned them easily. He believed that the last of these, astrology, was more important than the others, and he studied it so thoroughly that he could discover whatever might happen in the universe by the use of certain rules taught him by Virgil about the movement of the planets and the other stars, and by the appearance of the air. As we shall see, it was very fortunate that he learned this.

After Lucinius attained complete knowledge of all the arts, he also learned from Virgil the books of the poets and the philosophers. From there he next directed his mind's eye to a deeper knowledge of philosophy and obtained the name and reputation of a great philosopher. This was not done, however, without arousing the envy of many men. For those who could not attain to the highest understanding of knowledge envied him very much, and they took offense that the respect which was denied to them was paid to a young boy. Because of this they were trying to kill him by poison or some other way, but their fear of Virgil and the authority of the king's family checked their evil somewhat. But since envy always possesses and tortures its possessor and does not permit rest even for a moment, their hatred, which envy increased and goaded, could not be restrained longer.

Cunningly they decided to invite him to a banquet and mix poison with the wine. Long before this he had learned of their hatred for him by his knowledge of astrology, and he was not deceived. Nevertheless he cleverly feigned ignorance and said to them that it was neither fitting nor proper to have such an important banquet with such important guests without Virgil and the Roman nobility. He said if he came he would be happy to enjoy their generosity and he was ready, when the opportunity arose, to repay their kindness in turn. He assured them, however, that he did not dare to do anything at all without his teacher Virgil, who was his guardian and whose ferule he feared very much. When they heard this, blinded by their hatred, they invited Virgil and some other Roman citizens, not caring if they too died because of that deadly drink if only Lucinius did not escape their poisonous hands.

When the banquet began, each one reclined according to age and rank. Since Caesar had ordered everyone to honor Virgil, who was of the highest rank, he had the first place at the table. The one who had sent the invitations and who was the chief villain was conducting the banquet with the help of some others. Many dishes were served to the guests, different types of wine were drunk, and they feasted joyfully and abundantly. Meanwhile however, Lucinius, considering the aspects of astrology, was awaiting the drink they had mixed for him.

When the banquet was coming to an end and the guests had been cheered by all the food which human art could think of, suddenly that deadly, twisted snake, whom I called the chief villain, brought in a great, golden goblet filled with death and placed it before Virgil. At once the nostrils of those reclining were captivated by a sweet odor. The appetite of everyone was stimulated to drink. They all asked for the deadly potion. When it was offered to Virgil, Lucinius took the goblet and lifting his hand for silence said: "I fear this sweetness may contain some bitterness. The honeybee has a stinger, and to catch fish the fisherman puts bait on the hook."

They, whom the brand of their conscience confounded, were overcome with horror at these words. As the poet says, "Their face and color betrayed the crime."[14] Nevertheless, they tried to dissimulate and answer him. They said that the son of the king did not give them proper thanks when they honored him. He should not say such things, even in jest.

"I spoke not in jest," he said, "but in anger. You can prove that I and my friends were invited in good faith and that you are guiltless of this charge if you will take the first drink. Otherwise, I swear by the health of my father and of Caesar that you have plotted against our lives."

What could they do? Where could they turn? What could they answer to these charges? On all sides they were trapped, on all sides the noose was tightening, on all sides no hope of safety. They saw only two possibilities for themselves, one of which they could not avoid: either to drink or to die. But they did not know which of the two to choose. They knew that if they drank they would die; but if not, they would be handed over to Caesar as criminals to be tortured in many different ways. Nevertheless, they thought it better to die at their own hands than to expose themselves to the derision of others.

"O Lucinius," they said, "you will know that we plotted no evil against you or your friends if we live three days after we drink this wine."

He who had brought in the cup drank and then delivered it to his partners in crime to drink. They drank and, as the philosopher says, they fell into the pit which they had dug for others. They died there at the table with their eyes staring from their heads. So that famous boy by his diligence skillfully saved himself and his friends from death and took vengeance on the envious. Thus he acquired an outstanding reputation among noble and common people alike. No one dared to plot evil against him any more, nor did they even consider it, since all thought that one who had knowledge of the future was more than human.

Although Lucinius was considered so great by men, and although Virgil proclaimed that he was equal to him in every way, nevertheless he never was willing to sit in his presence or be considered his equal. He always remained under his ferule and discipline as if he were then learning the alphabet for the first time. His humility was especially attested by the fact that, although he was very tall and Virgil very small, whether he was walking or standing with his teacher his body was always stooped so that he might not seem taller or bigger than Virgil.

After Lucinius had been taught by Virgil for seven years he appeared second to no one in his knowledge of the arts and of philosophy. One day Virgil happened to go out to relieve himself. Lucinius remained alone in his room to study. He had barred the door and was reading Virgil's handbook, reviewing more thoroughly the rules of astrology. Suddenly in a fit of terrible emotion he shouted loudly and fell flat on the ground. When the terrified household heard this sound of agony, they ran up; the men and women from neighboring houses flocked together asking what had happened or what did the shout mean. Impatiently, as is the case with crowds, they broke open the door, ran into the room and saw Lucinius lying unconscious on the floor. They approached him and touched the limbs of his body, which were cold and stiff. Only around his heart did they feel a little heat and a slight pulse. By chance there was present in the crowd a man skilled in the art of medicine who knew that this unconsciousness was caused by grief and that the wind within the heart was surrounded and smothered by coagulated blood. He ordered that hot and cold water be brought to him immediately. When these were brought he bathed the extremities of the limbs with cold water and wrapped wool steeped in hot water around the heart like a plaster so that the heat of the watery element might dissolve gradually the coagulated blood. When dissolved, it would go through the limbs and restore their former functions, so that the wind freed from its prison would recover the free passageway of the arteries and restore motion to the body. He also placed near the nostrils scented spices to draw forth the wind and strengthen it. A half hour later Lucinius's natural color returned, as well as the heat and movement of his limbs. He arose and sat down, wondering at the number of people around him. The appearance of his countenance showed his grief and sadness.

While these things were happening, Virgil, unaware, was returning home accompanied by certain Roman philosophers and elders. At the very door of his house he received the sad news that his Lucinius had suddenly died. When he heard the words of his slave he was terribly upset. Although he was a man of great spirit and had been taught by the examples and deeds of brave men to balance the good and the bad on an equal scale he could not completely conceal his grief, which showed itself by intermittent sighs, broken speech, and welling tears. Although his manliness struggled with his love, and he concealed the greatness of his grief deep in his heart as best he could, yet a terrible sorrow raged widely and bitterly in his bosom. The tears in his eyes and his sobbing breath were a pent-up fire feeding on the neighboring fields.

At last, however, he entered his house of grief, as he thought, accompanied by the philosophers and the elders, thinking more about the funeral than hoping to find Lucinius alive. When he looked into the bedchamber he realized that, contrary to all expectation, the one he was mourning as dead was sitting up surrounded by a crowd of people. He also noticed the signs of grief and sadness on his pale face. When all except a few friends had departed from the chamber, he asked the cause of his sorrow. Lucinius, again sighing from the depths of his heart, replied, "O my illustrious master, at the ninth hour today when you left me to go walking, I happened to take up our book to memorize even more perfectly the rules of astrology. From the change of air on the first page I suddenly realized that my beloved mother had died and that my father Dolopathos had taken another wife. Even now he is sending ambassadors to take me back to be crowned king. I fainted because of the death of my mother and our coming separation. If human skill had not helped me, perhaps I would have died."

"I have known this for a long time," said Virgil. "I kept silent, however, lest I seem to be the author of your grief and sadness. But I congratulate you that you were wise enough to discover it for yourself. I rejoice to see that you are skilled in all knowledge and have risen through all the grades of philosophy. You must remember, however, that you learned the beginning of these arts from your friend Virgil. Although you are a king, although you are outstanding in the glory of your lineage, although you are my equal in the keenness of your knowledge and mind, yet it is proper that you obey him who gave you your divine soul as long as you live. And rightly so; for if the father must be loved and cherished by the son because he physically brought him weak and helpless into the world, so much more must the teacher, who furnishes knowledge of secret and holy things, be loved by the pupil. I have shown you an even greater thing, since I have flooded you with the light of divinity itself. You also know that I have concealed nothing, human or divine, from you, but rather disclosed these things to you word for word, as to a friend, not to a pupil. I am thankful that you have held them firmly in your quick mind. I am also thankful that I have been worthy of such a pupil, of whose perfection I can justly boast even to the greatest philosophers. I now ask that the love which has existed between us never be destroyed or broken by any passage of time. Let it be renewed day by day. Although we may be separated by many miles for a long time, let this love be bound in our hearts and minds always. When you go from me to claim your father's kingdom, show yourself to be a philosopher king and a king philosopher. Temper your kingly majesty with the training of philosophy, and entrust philosophy to the care of your kingly majesty. In all things strive to adapt yourself to all men as much as possible. Give to every age, sex, or condition the proper justice, and desire to be loved rather than feared. But so much for these things. You have been sufficiently instructed about them by Philosophy herself. Since you must now leave me in Rome and return to your country, please grant me one wish before you go."

"Can there be any wish so great which I would dare to deny you?" asked Lucinius. "Even if you asked my father's kingdom, I would gladly yield it. Come now, tell me what you wish."

"First," said Virgil, "you must swear to me by the welfare of your father and of Caesar that you will obey whatever I command."

He swore that he would obey any order, however difficult, if it were humanly possible.

"Then," said Virgil, "by the authority of your teacher I order you to speak no word from the time in which we are separated until you see me again. Not on the road, not in your country, not to the king, not to the queen, not to the nobles of your kingdom, not to anyone at all."

"Alas," said Lucinius, "who could obey such a terrible command? The tongue is the part of the body which is least controllable and most easily betrays us. What man in all the world with a tongue and the ability to speak could do this, unless he were a mute? Even the tongue of a mute moves, although to no purpose. But so be it. I shall go to my country obeying your orders, as is right. I shall put a rein on my tongue and guard my lips as if they were sealed with iron bars. But when my father greets me after my long absence, when the queen greets me, when the princes of the kingdom and noble ladies praise me to the stars, how can I check that restless and impatient part of the body? Will it not despise its prison and break into speech at the words of praise? You have ordered me to do the impossible."

"You swore, Lucinius," answered Virgil, "and you promised to obey. If you think my commands are worth anything at all, you will keep them. But if you despise them, I will not force you. Whether you obey me or not, I shall soon know."

Lucinius answered, "O illustrious teacher, I have always wished to obey your orders in all things. In this matter I shall do so, if it is possible."

While they were still in the chamber discussing this and other matters, there came at sunset the ambassadors of the king, who respectfully greeted Virgil, his friends, and his pupil on behalf of King Dolopathos. After Virgil had properly returned the greeting, they stated the orders of the king. In addition they brought gifts and a letter from the king in which the death of his mother and the desire of his father were announced.

"It would be easy," replied Virgil, "to obey the orders of the king, if I could return with Lucinius to his country. But I cannot go too far from Rome, since I am detained on some business of Caesar's. His departure is unbearable to me. The separation weighs upon me, but I cannot oppose the will of your master. Although I desire his continual companionship, yet I cannot hinder his happiness. But since you are going to set forth in the morning with the son of your master, let us spend the rest of the day and this night together in pleasure and conversation with fine food and drink." Then a banquet was held, and they feasted and talked until morning.

When the dawn gleaming with its golden rays poured its beams upon the earth, and the rising Lucifer bore witness that Phoebus Arctos was approaching, the ambassadors arose and covered their wagons with their kingly trappings. Mounting their horses they then departed from the city with Lucinius and Virgil and directed their course towards their country. Virgil went with them to a certain stream which flowed six miles from the city. There he stopped for the final farewell. Then they clasped each other, they embraced, they kissed, they matched groan with groan, sigh with sigh, tear with tear. When the strength of one failed he was restored by the other, and then the other took courage from the other. Who could count the sighs, the tears, the groans that burst from each breast? At last after a long time they said their final farewells. Virgil entrusted the half of his soul[15] to the ambassadors and returned to the city; but only half of him returned, since he had left part of his soul with Lucinius.

As Lucinius went his way, he showed by his sighs and tears how much he grieved at the separation, no less than Virgil. While the distance was gradually increasing each stopped and turned to feast his eyes with one last glance. Thus each one proceeded with hesitating step until a mountain intervened and robbed them of each other's sight. Then Virgil returned to the city and Lucinius to his native land.

Lucinius did not forget the command of his teacher and condemned himself to utter silence. When his friends spoke to him he answered not at all. They believed he was busy with his thoughts or grieving for his teacher, and so for that day and the next they refrained from speaking to him. They did not understand the situation at all. But he was still silent on the third day when they were approaching the borders of Sicily, and they became afraid that his silence and unrestrained grief might cause him to forget how to speak at all. They tried to arouse him with serious topics or with jokes; then they described the glory of the father and of the queen, the many nobles of the kingdom, and even the beauty of the women. When they realized that nothing, happy or sad, could break his deep silence, they truly believed that he had lost his senses as well as the use of his tongue. Then they were horrified beyond words and unmercifully began to tear their hair and rip their faces with their nails, lamenting in this way: "Alas! What can we do, how have we failed, what misery is ours, how did we deserve to go on this embassy? Woe, woe! We received from his teacher the son of our lord healthy and quite able to speak, but suddenly in our hands he has somehow become mute. How can we return his only son to his father mute, how can we have the audacity to meet his terrible gaze? Will he not torture us in many ways like criminals before the eyes of our friends, wives and children? He will think that we destroyed his son at the instigation of some enemy by poison or other evil means and will not even listen to our excuses. Would it not seem better and safer to flee and leave the son of the king in this city? But where can we go? How can we escape his presence? What place, what corner of the earth, what cave, what hiding place can conceal us? Even if we crossed the farthest oceans, if we went living into hell,[16] his power would drag us from there and bring us back as captives to his country. And there, before our friends, our wives, our children we would be set up for all to mock. O woe, woe! Wretchedly and miserably we have fallen into a noose from which we cannot be freed! On all sides we are beset! Everywhere we are surrounded by troubles! O death, which destroys happy men unexpectedly in a thousand ways, why do you pass us by in our misery? Why do you avoid those who desire you? O we would have been happy, we would have been thrice and four times blessed if six years ago we could have died nobly in some war in the service of our king. But our misery, our misfortune preserved us for this shame. Why is it not better to seek fleeing death with our own hands and swords and thus, perishing quickly, to free ourselves from the cruelty of the king and eternal shame?"

With these and other words the ambassadors, who had given up all hope, drew their naked swords to plunge them into their bodies. When Lucinius realized their purpose, he quickly threw himself at their feet and begged them with nods and signs not to commit an irrevocable act; shedding tears upon them and embracing them he relieved their grief as best he could. To make them feel safer and more secure he wrote on a tablet with his own hand and advised them not to seek death when they could live happily.[17] They were to fear nothing, since he would let his father know that they were not guilty. Perhaps the chain on his tongue would soon be loosened and he could speak. The ambassadors were somewhat reassured and hastened to go to the king as quickly as possible.

In the meantime Dolopathos had assembled at Palermo all the kings and nobles under his sway wishing them to be present at the coronation of his son, to offer him homage and fealty, and to receive their kingdom and honors from him. He had also gathered together in the same city supplies of grain and wine and all kinds of food imported by land and sea to feed all his guests. Who could judge the immense number of those who had come from kingdoms far and near? So great a number of soldiers and actors and dancers had come that so great a city and so great a palace could not hold even a third part of them. They had to live in tents scattered on the plains around the city.

When the ambassadors arrived in Sicily they came to a certain castle about ten miles from Palermo. After they had rested a while they informed the king, by messenger, of their arrival so that he and all the other kings and nobles could meet his son. When the king heard the news he was happy beyond words. He ordered the heralds to announce throughout the city that all the kings and nobles, with their sons of fourteen years or more, and all the soldiers, and all the noble ladies and maidens, festively attired, were to assemble on the next day outside the Roman Gate for the purpose of meeting his son, who was returning from his studies. He also announced that all the gold and silver and precious gems and tapestries in the city were to be placed along the Roman road from the gate to the palace, in honor of Lucinius. The road itself was paved with tapestries and silks of different colors so that the eyes of Lucinius would see nothing disagreeable or offensive. After the announcement the whole city echoed with voices. It was a sight to see the maidens dancing and the children playing. The applause for the actors and dancers, the melodies from the musical instruments rose on high. All prepared to meet Lucinius and eagerly awaited the morrow, especially the girls and boys, because they take the greatest delight in spectacles.

When Phoebus, happier than usual, had scattered the shadows of the dark night and, sprinkling his golden rays upon the lands, had illuminated the hoped-for tomorrow with his presence, all the people drove blessed sleep from their eyes and quickly prepared to meet Lucinius. The kings and nobles eagerly put on their purple robes and their golden crowns and their neck-chains. The ladies and the maidens adorned their faces with cosmetics to seem more beautiful. Zealously they attired themselves with all types of necklaces and ornaments imaginable and they preened before their mirrors. The young men and the squires were eager to bridle the horses and the mules of the kings and ladies with golden reins, and to cover them with silken trappings. When everything was arranged and ready, first the kings, then the nobles and the young soldiery mounted their horses and departed from the city. The ladies and the maidens followed them on their sumpter mules. Then they gathered together outside the Roman Gate and awaited the coming of King Dolopathos.

Suddenly the king himself, accompanied by his troops of soldiers and followed by a column of actors, dancers, and fluters fluting on their flutes, arrived on a horse worthy of its master. He himself was the most handsome of all the kings around him, clothed in purple, a jeweled diadem upon his head, a golden necklace around his neck, upon his thigh a sword. The queen was on his right, clothed in a gown of various golden shades and riding on a white mule. The daughters of the kings, girt in gowns with golden borders, followed and paid her honor.

When all who had come to meet the son of the king were gathered, they divided into three columns. In the middle column was the king with his kings and nobles and the glorious soldiers and the young men. The stately queen followed them with her entourage of ladies and maidens. In front of the king in the first column were the troupes of actors filling the air with music. Each column was a stade apart. Who could describe the pomp and display? Who could describe such riches, or the attire of the kings and nobles, or the haughtiness of the queen and her entourage of frolicsome matrons and maidens? Who could even describe the trappings of the horses? I think not the eloquence of Cicero nor even Homer with the nine Muses could do it. Let me pass over the gloriousness of the kings and the nobles and the women. All the equipment on the horses was of gold or silver or jewels or silk. The queen, her ladies and maidens could scarcely bear the weight of the gowns and necklaces, as the poet once said: "The girl was the least part of herself."[18]

In the meantime, those who had remained in the city were paving the road from the Roman Gate to the palace with different-colored tapestries. It was adorned on both sides with all the precious things in the city: all things beautiful to see or smell, all things of gold or silver, all things adorned with precious gems. Finally they clothed with the same gloriousness the palace itself and the temple of Jove, within and without.

King Dolopathos and his column advanced with stately pace, until they came into a certain wide plain two miles from the city. There he saw from afar his son nearing the column of actors. Immediately he spurred his horse and galloped through the middle of the plain until he came to his son, whom the troupe of actors was already greeting with music and song. Eagerly they embraced and exchanged kisses so long desired. The father kissed his son's honey-sweet mouth, then his tender features, then his eyes, which were like stars. Then you could see the kings, the nobles, the soldiers, and the youths struggling to be the first to greet Lucinius, to kiss him, and to pay homage with bowed heads. With the people thronging on every side, the father and the son retraced together the course to the city. The queen with her ladies and maidens had proceeded slowly, as women usually do, and were still at a distance. When they met those who were returning the queen first kissed Lucinius respectfully and all the other women did the same. Fear of a husband's jealousy restrained no one, nor did maidenly modesty prevent their offering pure and chaste kisses. The voices of all were lifted on high praising their gods who had given so great a successor to King Dolopathos. The sweet songs of the maidens, the games of the young men on horseback, and the dulcet voices of the actors made the joyful hearts of all even more joyful. With this gloriousness, with this display, Lucinius was led into the city like a triumphing general. He himself had not forgotten his oath. His attitude was the same to all. His face was happy, and he responded to everyone without a word but by only a movement of the lips, a motion of the eye, or a nod of the head. In such an uproarious throng no one could notice his silence.

When those who had remained in the city heard that Lucinius was near they ran to meet him with flowers and olive branches, shouting and saying: "Glory, praise, and honor to our future king, the son of Dolopathos!" So with the praises of those before and behind, with lutes, cymbals and psalteries, songs and harps and every kind of music, he entered the city on the road paved with gold, jewels, and silks, which led to the palace. O with what great gloriousness, with what great display of riches was he received! You would have thought all the riches of the world had flowed there, all the gold from the sands of the Pactolus, every jewel and gem found in India, all the treasures of Alexandria. But why should I try to tell of each thing? It would be impossible. Even Rome, the mistress of the world, never received one of her consuls with such great gloriousness, such great pomp, such great display, not even Octavian when he returned triumphant over Cleopatra. The sun itself, as if it were a slave to Lucinius, shone upon the earth more brilliantly than usual. The rays of its light, gleaming on the mass of gold and silver and gems, reflected so strongly that it forced those looking to turn away their eyes.

Then the procession came to the temple of Jove where the father thanked the gods for the safe return of his son after so long a time. After he had slaughtered many victims, he ordered all to go to their homes or tents. He and Lucinius with the royal family went to the palace, which had been clothed with gold and jewels and tapestries. Lucinius, indeed, who bore the command of Virgil like a mark on his brain, guarded his tongue. He replied to all the greeting and applause by a movement of the eyes or a nod of the head without speaking. On that day his father did not notice this since his thoughts and feelings were completely occupied with unspeakable joy. No one else noticed, except the ambassadors, who knew the situation.

But when Phoebus had run his course and dipped into the western waves; when night, ordained for the sleep and quiet of men, casting its shadows before it, had arrived, King Dolopathos and his queen retired to their bedchamber. Lucinius was led to another chamber by young maidens appointed for the task. There, tired from the celebration, he took his rest and refreshed his spirits with pleasing sleep. Dolopathos, who was thinking about the morrow's preparation, did not sleep at all that night. Rising at dawn he went to the bedchamber of his son to tell him his hopes and plans and to discover the reaction of Lucinius. When the attendants were sent out of the room, he bolted the door, awoke his son, greeted him with a kiss, and said:

"How the world is controlled, or to what blind and uncertain fate the race of man is subject, I realize that you know best of all, my dearest son. As you know, the world is fleeting and inconstant. It subjects its lovers to unpredictability. It permits some men to overcome others. It favors this man over that man. It deprives us of honors or wealth and levels us to the dust. Those it exalts beyond measure it hurls into ruin. With what fickleness, with what inconsistency does Fortune mock even kings and nobles who for some reason are born to riches and mastery. At times she exalts them with happiness, at times she casts them into adversity and afflicts them with various miseries. At times she raises them to the highest glory, at other times she reduces them to the deepest poverty.

> The judge makes a mockery of justice,[19]
> All mankind hangs by a slender thread,
> And the strong fall unexpectedly.[20]

Devouring death itself is hostile to the nature of man.

> Death with equal foot strikes the towers
> of kings and the huts of the poor.[21]

Neither king nor pauper is spared. She fears not purple robes, nor houses filled with gold and silver. Lofty towers, though placed on mountain tops, do not shut her out. She destroys without distinction the king amid his purples and gold as well as the poor man living in a hovel. And alas! when a strong man thinks he is going to live longer and do more, then death unexpectedly seizes him.

> The fates are envious and great men fall in a little while.[22]

Today a king sits on his throne like a god and men revere him. If he dies tomorrow those same men will shudder at his stinking carcass. Since, therefore, we see such treachery and mutability in life, and no man knows his end, it has seemed to me to be a wise move to anticipate your future and the future of the kingdom of Sicily, while I am still alive and my ship sails with favorable winds. When death carries me away, you will be secure in power, and the state will remain at peace. Great kings have always worried about this, and only when it has been settled are they happy and worthy of praise. This is my wish, and therefore I have summoned you to establish you as my successor before I die. This is my intention, my plan, my hope, the desire of my heart. Up to this point I, with the help of the gods, have been fortunate in the glory of the world and the administration of the kingdom. But now I am weary and old, my spirit is enfeebled, my strength fails, my courage is going, my limbs tremble, my body is weak, I see that nothing remains for me except a tomb. And so I abdicate. I give to you the honor of the kingdom and the burden of that honor. Interrupt your study of philosophy and consider the affairs of your father's kingdom. Let a stronger man take the throne of his strong father, let a more fortunate man succeed his fortunate father. Make my deeds more famous by your greater ones!"

While his father was speaking these and other words Lucinius was listening, but he kept absolute silence. When his father noticed this he said, "My son, what is it? Why are you silent? Does my intention seem right or wrong to you? Are you pleased or displeased? My son, tell me your wish. What do you think?"

When he remained silent his father was offended and became angry. Lucinius embraced and kissed him again and again and showed by signs that he could not speak at all. When his father realized this he was astounded and amazed. "When you were seven years old," he said, "you could speak your mother tongue perfectly. Now, when you are fifteen, have you become mute? Did that mother of eloquence, rhetoric, take care of you in this way? What is it? What has happened if you are really mute? Or do you scorn my words and mock my old age? Do you think me unworthy of a reply?"

While he was saying these things, he kept shaking his head to and fro grievously and striking his hands together. Lucinius, humbly and simply, threw himself down and kissed his father's feet and hands and his venerable white hair, showing in this way that his silence was not contempt of his father but necessity. Even this increased the father's grief so that he shouted that the cause of this disaster was himself, or Virgil, or the ambassadors.

"Woe to me!" he cried. "Why did I decide to send my only son from me? I myself am the cause of this grief. O Virgil, where is your pretended friendship, where is your faith? Did you teach your friend's son only to return him mute? But who would think this? Who would believe that you would bring this harm upon the son of Dolopathos and the nephew of Caesar? Yet, maybe those damned ambassadors did this! O Virgil, when your guardianship was removed, they were bribed by someone to destroy my son! O damned criminals, poisoners who will die a thousand deaths! Where are the crosses, where are the whips, where are the torturers of Sicily? O if I only had a bronze bull to put them in and fire to put under it to show them as a horrible spectacle to everyone!"[23]

When Lucinius saw the terrible grief of his father and realized he was preparing to kill the ambassadors, he took a tablet and pen and ink and wrote that he did not scorn his father's old age, nor had he been harmed by Virgil or the ambassadors, but that his affliction came from grief when he heard the news about the death of his mother.[24] He thus freed his teacher and the ambassadors from suspicion of the crime.

While these things were going on in the bedroom, the friends of the king had come to the palace to consult about the coronation of Lucinius. They inquired for the king and learned that he had gone to his son's chamber at dawn. Approaching the door, they knocked confidently and requested that he open for his friends. When the king heard that his friends were there he rose quickly and sadly opened the door. When he saw his friends he began to weep again. Tears streamed from his eyes and down his face. The grief, the groans, the sobs began once more. His confused friends stood thunderstruck. They were stupefied at the strangeness of the situation and they wondered at the change. They wanted to know what had happened and how such sadness had taken the place of his former joy. Then the king said, "O my good friends, you who have been sharers of my happiness up to this point, hear how my lute has been changed to lamentation and my song to words of grief."[25]

He told them, step by step, the misfortune of his son. His friends tried to console him, advised him to call upon his innate strength and not consume his soul with sorrow. They said they would try to make his son speak again and added that physicians believed that contraries were cured by contraries. "Now, then," they said, "take our advice and lay aside your grief. Order the court to be postponed for seven days. Meanwhile show your son all the joys and delights that can be thought of. Let him hear only the beauty of sweet music. Let beautiful maidens stand near to hum sweet melodies and, with gesture and touch, with kisses and embraces, summon him to the game of love. Feed him pleasant food and every day make him tipsy with strong drink. Let nothing ugly or gloomy strike his eyes, but only happy and pleasant things. In this way when happiness has been implanted in his heart, his sadness will be relieved and gradually abolished completely. Then his former ability to speak will return."

At this point the queen, who had heard that the king was mourning, interrupted. When she learned the cause of the grief and the advice of his friends she voluntarily offered her help. She said that she would take Lucinius into her own bedchamber and show him whatever the friends had advised. She promised that she would give him back the power to speak. The king, who believed the advice of his friends was good, was consoled. He thanked the queen for her offer and swore by the gods that if she could do what she promised he would give half of his kingdom to her. So he entrusted Lucinius to the queen and told the kings and nobles that the coronation could not take place for seven days because of some business matters.

The queen took Lucinius and surrounded him with her maidens, laboring carefully to accomplish what she had promised the king. She chose from the entire city the most beautiful virgins who knew how to sing and play musical instruments and added them to her court. She ordered them, beautifully adorned, to stand near Lucinius night and day and to summon him to pleasure and the game of love in any way they could. She decreed that maidenly modesty should hinder no one, that no one should conceal her bosom or her other charms from him.

They bathed carefully and adorned their bodies with various cosmetics and perfumes and splendid garments and stayed near Lucinius and tended him as the queen had ordered. They tried to arouse him to the game of love, sometimes by the sweet sound of the lute, sometimes by songs or words of love, sometimes by embraces. Sometimes their wanton hands even touched him where he was most responsive. Violets, roses, lilies, the garlands on the bed, all urged him to the sport. Even the queen, covered with gold and jewels, sat near and urged him to enjoy the maidens. To bring joy more easily to his heart and make him more prone to love she tried to make him tipsy with strong drink, since she knew that wine makes a man happy and talkative and that drunken men are quick to speak and to love.

How did that wonderful young man act among the snakes and flames of lust? Placed in the fire, did he not burn? Did he not yield to the craftiness of all these maidens, whom I rightly called snakes (for there is no cunning beyond the cunning of the serpent, nor evil beyond the evil of woman)? Who is made of such iron that he would not soften at such embraces, at such kisses? Whose heart, even if made of adamant, could remain whole? Who is made of such rock, whose flesh so unfeeling as not to be titillated at their wanton touches? And no wonder! Does not the beauty and carnal knowledge of women deceive and cheat even philosophers? But that young man, so strong, so chaste, knew why this was done. He knew that the skill of woman is stronger than all skills. He firmly decided that for his father's sake he would endure all their allurements up to the point of the actual game of love, thinking it would be a glorious and safe thing for him if he, a young man, overcame what had conquered many old men. He knew that if he yielded in this one thing he must break the promise to his teacher. Therefore he was always cheerful and endured their embraces, their kisses, their touches, but in bed at the final moment he behaved like a senseless stone. In this way the queen and her maidens spent two days in vain.

The queen, who was angry that the youth made light of her attentions, decided to take a more active role in the seduction rather than not obtain the king's promise. She arrayed herself more beautifully than usual and adorned her bosom with jewels, her hands with rings, her neck with necklaces. She painted her face with cosmetics made of milk and roses and wore a special gown. She put on a golden coronet and permitted her golden hair to flow freely down her back. If you had seen her so dressed and adorned, you would have thought her another Helen for whom the entire East could rightly go to war a second time. Compared to her lustre, the lily was black; compared to her blush, the rose was pale. Armed with such adornment, such beauty, she shut her maidens out of the bedchamber and approached the helpless youth, who was protected only by the weapons of his chastity. She made her attack on all sides with soft words and suggestive questions. She brandished the fiery darts of Cupid, she brought up her catapults and tried to overthrow that strong citadel of his heart. Sometimes she licked and pressed and sucked his lips. Sometimes, glancing at him with her wanton eyes and moving her limbs, she summoned him to war and the battle of love. But he opposed the shield of his chastity to her darts and catapults and repelled them bravely. She did not hesitate but pressed on even more eagerly.

The siege continued in this way all day and all night. At last, however, the besieger was captured, the huntress became the prey. While she kept gazing upon the beautiful complexion of the youth, upon his laughing eyes and golden hair, upon his hands and arms and other gifts of nature (Nature, the artisan of man, had omitted nothing of her riches), while, I say, she kept looking at these things, suddenly she was seized by a blind and insane lust and she burned completely with passion for Lucinius. From this time she did not use vague words or hints but put aside all shame. Nakedly and openly with words, kisses, embraces, even by handling his manhood without restraint she commanded him to satisfy her lust.

In the meantime, however, she told the king to be of good cheer, saying that Lucinius was doing well. The youth, thinking she was not so shameless as insane, kept repelling her with the greatest horror and indignation. To no purpose. She burned with a greater fire of lust and violently renewed the attack on every occasion. At each repulse she was in agony. She even had recourse to more powerful aids such as charms and drugs. She had a potion made from the juice of herbs and gave it to him to drink. But Lucinius had foreknowledge of all things. He shielded his ears against her poisonous incantations, and he would not drink the love potion. When she realized she could not overcome him in this way, she returned to the use of prayers and tears. She proclaimed herself the unluckiest and most wretched of mortals who endured such things for her love. He was not moved by prayers and complaints, nor was he bent by her wanton tears.

Finally the queen realized that she could prevail in no way at all, but her passion continued to feed on her vitals. She summoned the women of her court, who knew all her secrets, and spoke to them with these words: "Oh, you who know my secrets and share my happiness, when I was trying to please the king and do his service, while I was stretching my hand to a drowning man, so to speak, carelessly I fell into the deep. So I did not save him, but I destroyed myself. I pitied the king's sorrow for his son and promised that I would restore his speech. I have not fulfilled my promise but am like the traveler who warmed a frozen snake in his bosom and was destroyed by it.[26] I burn with so much passion, I am tortured so much by his beauty that nothing else in all the world seems beautiful to me, nothing sweet, nothing pleasant, except him. I cannot sleep, I cannot rest. The sweet taste of food is bitter and disgusts me. My heart yearns for him, my eyes look for him. I cannot help myself. I have begged, I have wept, I have tried to move him to pity my complaints. I even used the juice of herbs, charms, drugs. But to no purpose. All these things affect him no more than straw. His heart is adamant and his breast is iron. Tears, prayers, herbs, charms, drugs are of no avail. He cares not for my nobility nor my beauty, but despises me like a slave working in a mill. Yet my love does not grow cold from this insult, but, blazing higher and higher, feeds without remission upon my body. Sometimes even

> my senses abide no more in their firm seat,
> nor does my color remain unchanged; the moist
> tear glides stealthily down my cheek and shows
> the lingering fires by which I am devoured.[27]

What shall I do? What more can I plan? What hope is now left for me? I shall die if I cannot obtain my wish. But the sun will change its course more easily than the hardness of his heart. So I must die."

As the queen was pouring forth these things brokenly and without restraint, as lovers do, one of the women who was a close friend of hers, pretending great indignation, burst into invective against him. "O most foolish and wretched of all women, you who have lowered yourself to such shame and indignity as to offer your beauty and your nobility to a mute and senseless log. Even if he had sense and the use of his tongue like other men, yet we should consider him hateful. His father brought him here to place a ruler upon your back and disinherit you and your sons, if you ever have any, from the kingdom of Sicily. Are you sick and tormented by the love and comeliness of one who, as long as he lives, will bring shame and loss upon you and yours, especially when he completely despises your immodesty? Change your attitude! Renew your strength! Let us all hasten to destroy this enemy. Tomorrow when the kings and nobles have gathered in the palace, you, dressed as usual, must go alone to Lucinius. There, in his presence, with your fingernails tear your clothes, your face, and your hair. Loudly shout for help. When we hear your voice we too shall run in and also lacerate ourselves. When we have roused the whole palace we shall say that the son of the king tried to pollute the bed of his father by raping you. Then you, mangled and torn, must go to the king and throw yourself at his feet. There, before the kings and nobles, demand justice for such a crime. Strengthen your mind; do not fear a mute. Your father is here as well as your kingly brothers. Your friends are here. Our fathers are kings and nobles who will strongly defend you."

When that servant of Medea had spoken, the mind of the queen, once weak with love, began to rage so madly against Lucinius that her hatred was greater than the passion with which she had burned before. Her love was changed to cruelty and madness. Truly as the poet says: "Woman is always a varied and changing thing."[28] In less than an hour what she had wanted she scorned, she hated what she had loved, what she had offered she denied, she attacked what she had fled.

> She dissolves in laughter and weeps bitter tears.[29]

Everything was reversed. But why go on? When morning came she went to Lucinius as she had been instructed, and before his eyes she ripped her face with her nails and rent her hair with her hands. Her blood flowed freely and stained her dress. She ripped her garments and with great cries alarmed and aroused the palace. Her conspirators in crime gathered together. Their shouts increased the uproar. They mangled themselves and ripped their clothes, their faces, their hair. O what are you doing, Medea? O more savage than Medea, fiercer than Clytemnestra and most shameless of all women, what are you doing? Do you mangle yourself to kill an innocent youth? Will you attack him because he refused your lust? Does chastity deserve so little? Where is that love with which you burned? Where are the tears, where are the prayers, where are the embraces, where are the wanton kisses? Whence now such great hatred? But, as the philosopher says, "the result of hatred and of insane love is the same." This is the insanity of woman, this is her audacity. When she cannot overcome she goes mad and dares to commit any impiety.

The kings and nobles had gathered in the palace with Dolopathos to consider some business about the kingdom. When they heard the shouts and the uproar they did not know what it meant. But suddenly that venomous snake with her horde of lesser snakes came from her cave. There she was, with disheveled hair, torn cheeks, spattered with her own blood, her clothing ripped down to the navel. With sad steps she approached the king and throwing herself at his feet asked all to hear her. When the king and the others saw the strange appearance of the queen they were overcome with grief and anger. King Dolopathos raised the queen and ordered her to tell quickly who had dared to commit such an impious deed. At first she pretended great grief and sighed and groaned and wept so that these pretensions might lend greater faith to her words. Then she said, "O most just King, out of respect for you, I and the women of my court took over the care of your son and labored night and day in every way to restore him to you sound of mind and able to speak. I thought we had accomplished this when I joyfully discovered that he was speaking pleasantly and dining with us. But today I discovered that the reason was not grief for his dead mother, or sadness for his absent teacher, but treachery! Today, when he found me alone in the bed chamber, realizing that he had discovered an opportunity for his crime, like an unbridled stallion (I blush to say it) he leaped upon me to defile me with rape. Cursing the crime I tried to repel the attack of his lust as best I could. When he found he could not obtain his desire by pleading or violence, with all his strength he ripped my face with his fingernails, as you can see. I realized that my strength could not restrain his lust, and I could do nothing else but shout for help. These women ran in to help me and free me from the madman. Since he could not overpower me he turned his madness against them and wounded them in the same way. We could have taken vengeance upon him, but out of respect we preferred to restrain our wrath and bring our complaint to you. Now before all your nobles, O King, I ask justice and judgment from you for this terrible crime." When she had said this she was silent.

Scarcely able to restrain himself until the queen had finished, the king jumped up and roared like a lion: "O immortal gods, O Jupiter, O Apollo, O Mercury, O Juno, O Venus, why have you unjustly declared war upon me? Why do you torture your worshipper with unexpected grief? Up to this time you have permitted me to live a happy life; up to this time you have been kind to me. But suddenly, unjustly, my life is ending miserably. I have always piously worshipped your temples, altars, and statues; I have glorified you with sacrifices; I have beautified you with adornments more than all the kings of my time. By my prayers and tears I obtained from you a son, whom I had so long hoped for and awaited. Why do you now, repenting the gift, enviously take him away after he has been nobly born, well brought up, and well educated? But O woe! Why do I blame the benign gods? Should we not rather consider the guilt of my son and of my misery? The gods are just. I am wretched, and my son a blasphemer! All you kings and nobles, glory and the strength of my kingdom, consider and see if there is any grief like mine.[30] I reared and educated my son, whom I had decided to exalt over all. But he scorned me so much that he has committed a crime against me which they say has never been committed against a father."

While he lamented in this way, his son, calm and serene, came and stood before his father. All wondered if one with such a guileless countenance could have committed so great a crime. When Dolopathos saw his son, his great grief increased; he renewed his lamentation and was more deeply wounded. "Son," he said, "I wish you had never been born. I wish your birth had never made me so happy. You have afflicted me with so much evil, so much shame. Indeed, the astrologers were wrong, the prophets were liars who said that you would ascend the throne and worship some mighty god. They also prophesied that you would do no evil. Their only correct prediction was that you would be a wise philosopher and suffer treachery from your enemies; nor was their art wrong in this. How can they be wrong in other things when they spoke the truth about this? Or is this the treachery they predicted?"

At this the queen burned with a greater fire and pressed more madly to the attack. She swore to the gods that in the future she would never consider him her king, never lie with him again, until he gave her complete justice for the insult. Her father, her brothers, her relatives, kings and nobles who were there, stood forth boldly and declared their anger at the queen's misfortune. They demanded that her insult be avenged, especially when the king seemed to suspect treachery and not to trust her clothes, and wounded face, and flowing blood. These things would have been enough to accuse Lucinius of the crime even if the queen had remained silent. Lucinius, himself, who had a clear conscience, did not say a word to his father or to them. He did not change color or expression, so that all were forced to wonder.

Imagine, O reader, how great a tumult and conflict then arose in the mind of the king when justice forced him to punish the crime but paternal affection inclined him to pity. What could he do, since he was both a father and a king? The one demanded pity, the other judgment. At last, however, love yielded to justice, and the king ordered his nobles to pass sentence how his son must be punished. They received the king's permission for a little delay and went to a secret place where they consulted all the chapters of the Roman laws. It was discovered that he must be burnt alive. But what man who has sons and knows the love that exists between father and son would pass such a terrible sentence on a king's only son? Each one feared to incur the hatred of the king. Each one also considered that if such a misfortune should ever happen to him he would also have to undergo a similar sentence. Even those who had taken the side of the queen and who had recently been so enraged trembled like weak and shaking fawns at the approach of a lion. When they finally returned to the king no one dared to make the sentence known. All pleaded ignorance saying that the laws had decreed nothing about such a matter. They asked to be relieved of their task and suggested that the king punish his son in any manner and as much as he wished. This, they said, would satisfy them.

The king, however, realized that their reluctance was not because of ignorance but fear. He swore by the gods that if anyone told him what he had found he would not deprive that one of his friendship or rank. He swore he would not move from that spot until they had passed sentence on his son. Again and again they made excuses to the king. As he kept forcing them, however, at last they disclosed what the laws had decreed about such a crime. The king approved the sentence. He ordered a herald to go throughout the city announcing that everyone, men and women, the highest and the lowest, noble and commoners, kings and princes, was to meet outside the city on a certain plain. Everyone was ordered to carry wood and straw.

When morning came all the people, great and small, bearing bundles of logs and kindling, met on the designated plain and there piled up their burdens. Who can imagine how great a pile was there when more than two hundred thousand men had put down their logs! Dolopathos with his kings and nobles and the queen with her court arrived at the place on foot, carrying kindling. In the right hand he carried a torch, in the left a bundle of straw. Calm, silent, unhesitant, feet naked, hands tied behind his back, clothing stripped from his body, like an innocent lamb, Lucinius was led to the punishment.

When they had arrived at the place, the king with his own hand put the torch to the wood. Immediately the fire spread, licking the kindling and the straw and the dry wood until it covered everything. The flames rose to the sky, the smoke obscured the very air, a horrible sight. The king ordered his son to be thrown into the flames, but from all that crowd not one was found who dared to lay a hand on him. Everyone believed such an order to be more cruel than just. But what terrible grief gripped the heart of the father when he ordered this! What terrible sorrow lacerated the souls of his friends when they heard it! The people were amazed at such a change of fortune, they trembled at his ill luck. They were stunned that such misery had followed such glory, and they grieved that he who was to be their king was about to die.

While the king kept repeating his order and all refused, suddenly the crowd parted and an old man of reverend face, thick beard, and white hair rode up to the king on a white mule. He carried an olive branch as a sign of peace in his right hand. Dismounting from his mule, he reverently greeted the king and all who were there. The king replied cordially and asked his country, his race, how he happened to be there, where he came from, and where he was going. "O King," he replied, "I am a Roman by birth and nation, and I am called one of the seven wise men. It is my custom to travel the world, to visit cities, castles, and villages. I go to the courts of kings and nobles and bring the judgments, the examples, and the cases of the ancients to the notice of the living. I am glad to learn what I do not know, and I teach what I have learned."

"I need at this time the advice and help of wise men," replied Dolopathos, "because today there are no wise men in the kingdom of Sicily."

The wise man said, "If it is not contrary to Your Majesty's will, I would like to know who that handsome young man is, what crime he has committed, and what that fire signifies."

The king admitted that it was his only son. He told how he had become mute, why he was entrusted to the queen, by whom he had been accused, and how the sentence had been found by his nobles.

The wise man said, "When a father kills his only son, it would seem to be an example of too much cruelty or too much justice. But since it is my duty to give you an ancient precedent from the treasury of my heart (I do this to all the kings and nobles whom I happen to meet), order all these people to pay close attention." The king obeyed and "all grew silent and intent"[31] while they watched and listened. The wise man stood on a hill and began.

The Story of the First Wise Man

The Dog

There was, O King, a certain young man of noble birth, as mortals consider such things, who wished to avoid the reputation of greediness lest it detract from his nobility. He even tried to put his reputation on a par with the greatest. So he began to spend the inheritance left him by his parents more wastefully than wisely.

He was easily moulded to vice, harsh to his advisors, slow to foresee the useful, wasteful of his money, proud and greedy and fickle.[32]

He desired to increase his followers of servants and knights, often to wear expensive clothing, and "to enjoy horses and new arms and the sport of the sunny field."[33] Without limit he gave his money to everyone who asked, especially to actors and dancers whose art and skill he admired. After a while his friends and relatives became worried, tried to restrain him by reproofs and warnings, but he considered their warnings and advice proof that they were jealous of his fame and glory and paid no attention at all. After a few years spent in wasteful living he exhausted his chattels and began to drain his estate. While he was doing these things his reputation became famous among people throughout the world. But if you always take and put back nothing, you can exhaust the "bottomless pit."[34] He always spent and never saved, so in a short time he lost his inheritance and his father's estate. He had no more to give, and no one gave. At last, sick and sorry, he was forced to recognize his stupidity. But it was too late.

So, O King, when he desired to seem glorious and powerful beyond his means, he lost his means and the glory which he had improperly assumed. He fell into the depths of poverty. All the flatterers, who formerly had praised him to the skies, stopped their praises when the gifts stopped. No one visited him, no one paid him any respect. His friends and relatives, whose good advice he had despised for so long, would not even look at him. When he realized that he was placed on the lower rim of fortune's wheel, and that he was a burden and a mockery to friends and strangers, he decided to leave his country and travel to unknown lands. He thought it would be better to be wretched among strangers than among people he knew, since someone has said, "Lonely places make the wretched happy."[35]

And so, O King, ready to go wherever fortune might call, he secretly left his home in the dead of night, taking nothing with him except his wife, his little son in its cradle, a horse, a dog, and a hawk. This was all he had left. After he had wandered through many lands, cities, and villages, he came to a city in a country he had never visited before. The sun was setting when he entered the city and stopped in a certain square, not knowing where to go. One of the citizens saw him and realized he was a foreigner. He approached him, asked him who he was, where he came from, and the purpose of his visit. He told him his complete situation and added that he would gladly stay in the city if he could only find some lodging. The citizen felt sorry for him. "I have," he said, "a stone building which no one has lived in for five years. You may live there as long as you like." The offer was gratefully accepted. They went to the house, he received the keys and moved in.

The knight remained in the city and every day went hunting for food with his dog or his hawk. This was his only means of support. His noble birth would not permit him to live like a farmer or a laborer or a beggar. As I said, he went hunting every day while his hungry wife remained at home, and often brought back to his wife a hare or a crane or some such thing. If he ever returned with nothing, they remained hungry until the evening of the following day, or until he caught something. It happened one day that he caught nothing and the next morning he set out without having eaten. He left his dog at home and hunted for food on horseback with the hawk. When he did not return after a long time, his wife, who could not bear a two days' fast, was forced to go to the house of a woman nearby to ask for food. While she was away and her husband was hunting, a great snake came out of a hole in the wall of the old stone building and tried to kill the little son, who had been left at home. When the dog saw this he broke the rope which tied him and fought with the snake, killed it, and, seizing it with his teeth, dragged it far away from the little boy. During the fighting, however, the cradle had been over-turned so that the face of the child was looking down upon the pave-ment. Suddenly the knight, returning with his prey, entered the house, saw the overturned cradle, the bloody dog, and the pavement all stained with blood. He thought, of course, that the famished dog had eaten his little son and that his wife had fled. In a fit of rage and madness he killed the horse and the dog with his sword and tore the hawk to pieces. As he was about to kill himself with his own sword, his wife returned. She righted the cradle and began to suckle her son. Then they found the dead snake and realized the faithfulness of the dog. The knight was sorry for what he had done, but it was too late.

"Take note, O King, how that hasty anger injured him when he im-petuously killed the things by which he lived. Lest you perhaps do something for which you are sorry, do not summarily carry out this sentence. Take my advice, and go over the laws again and again. Perhaps you will find something undiscovered which will free your son. And because I have given you an example from my treasury, in-stead of favors or gifts, I ask that you permit your son to live the re-mainder of this day. During this period if some better solution can be found and he can live, your joy and profit will be great. But if not, tomorrow will be soon enough to carry out your commands."

The king said, "Since you have told me an amazing story and one that I have not heard before, I cannot deny your request." So the king and his son and all the people returned to the city, and the wise man went his way.

The king ordered the sentence to be reconsidered. Advice was sought, the laws were again consulted, but nothing else was found. When morning came the king had the herald summon all the people with the kings and the nobles, the queen and his son. Everyone returned to the place of punishment carrying logs or kindling. When the fire had been started again the father ordered his son to be cast into the flames, but no one dared to do it.

Suddenly an old man of venerable appearance, sitting on a large ass, came through the multitude straight to the king. In his hand he carried an olive branch. He greeted the king and all those present cordially. When the greeting was returned by the king, he asked what the gathering of the people meant, what was the meaning of the naked youth, and what the fire signified. The king told the crime of his son and the sentence of the nobles, and in turn asked the old man who he was, where he came from, and what had impelled him to come there. He replied, "I am a Roman citizen and I am called one of the seven wise men. It is my custom to spend my life visiting the courts of kings and nobles, and going to cities, villages and castles. I investigate the judgments, the laws, and the customs of all places, and I tell to those who listen the good and bad fortunes of men. I always learn, I always teach. Since I move from place to place, chance brought me here, I was not impelled. But I cannot wonder enough that you have the heart to permit your only son, so handsome and so wise, to be burnt alive, no matter what he has done. But before I leave, I shall give you a gift which I also give to other kings. I shall tell you what happened once, if you will let me be heard." All were silent at the order of the king and the wise man, standing on a hill, began.

The Story of the Second Wise Man
The Treasure[36]

Long ago there was a certain great and powerful king who diligently collected treasure and filled to the top a tower of great height with gold and silver and every precious thing. He had a knight whose trust he had tested in many ways and to him he gave the keys of the treasury. For many years the knight guarded the treasury, but after he was worn out with work and old age and could no longer bear the confusion and worry of the court, he firmly requested the king to take back the keys of the treasury and thus spare his weakness and old age. He said that he wished permission to return home and spend the rest of his life quietly and happily with his sons. The king thought that his request was reasonable and, after he had given him many gifts, regretfully permitted him to retire. The keys and the treasury were entrusted to the charge of another man. The knight returned home and took charge of the affairs of his household.

He had many sons, the oldest of whom was of military age. Since his father loved him very much he gave him all his wealth and told him to spend it lavishly to obtain fame and friends for himself. The son used his father's estate immoderately and extravagantly. He was eager to get horses, weapons, clothes, and other things which young men value and take pleasure in. Thus his gifts bought many friends who quickly depart when the gifts are gone. In a short time his father's money box was empty, and he returned home to complain that he had no money. Then his father realized he had done the wrong thing and was sorry. "My son," he said, "since I foolishly loved you too well, I gave you all I had. But you galloped at full speed and forgot restraint. Everything is gone so that now only my home is left. What more can I do? I am sorry that you have lost your reputation and good name at your age, but I cannot help you. Yet if you wish to live on your former scale I have a plan, although a dangerous one. Do you dare to go with me in the dead of night to the tower which contains the king's treasure?"

When the son heard this, he said, "Father, I would refuse to undergo no danger with you, however perilous, if only I can be wealthy. If I am not wealthy the glory of my name is also gone." (See, O King, how he did not hope for glory obtained by virtue, but tried to gain it by money or theft.)

They both arose in the night, went to the tower, and knocked a hole in the wall with iron sledges. The father entered. After he had taken as much treasure as he wished, he left and covered the hole. They returned to their home burdened with another's wealth, and the young man again enjoyed his extravagance. Whenever he needed more wealth they returned to the treasury.

It happened, however, that the king desired to see his treasure. He summoned the guard, entered the tower, and saw that a great part of it had been stolen. Although he was full of rage he concealed it. On his return he went to a certain weak, old man to ask his advice. This old man had at one time been a famous bandit whom the king had caught and put out his eyes. The king had permitted him to eat every day at his own table, and he often gave good, sound advice to the king. He was a man who had seen and had heard much and had learned by experience. The king told him about his loss and asked how he could recover his treasure. The old man gave the following advice. "O King," he said, "if you wish to discover whether your own guard or another did this, order that a bundle of green grass be placed over a fire and put in the tower. Seal up every opening, walk around the tower again and again to see if you can see smoke coming out from a chink in the wall. When this is done return to me, and I shall advise you what must be done next."

The king ordered the old man's instruction carried out immediately. When this was done he closed all openings and began to walk around the tower. Inside the tower, the heat of the fire and green grass suddenly produced much smoke, which filled the tower to the top. Since there were no other air holes it went out through the hole which had been blocked up again, but without cement. Seeing this, the king quickly returned to the old man and told him what he had seen.

When he had heard this, the old man said, "You realize, O King, that robbers have taken your treasure through the hole where the smoke came out. They will take away the rest unless you catch them by some trick. As long as they are successful they will not stop until they have drained the entire treasury. I suggest that you conceal your loss. Keep silent, and in this way no rumor will come to the ears of the people and reveal your concern to the thieves. Meanwhile, fill a wide, deep vat with hot asphalt, resin, pitch, and glue. Place this inside the tower just below the hole so that when the thief, without knowledge of the trap, returns in his usual way to the treasury he will suddenly fall into the vat where he will be caught and stuck in the glue. Whether he wishes it or not, on the next day he will be exposed."

The king was amazed at the clever plan of the old man. He put a vat filled with boiling glue at the hole, locked up the tower, and departed. The deadly day which passes by no man, good or evil, brought the poor father with his son to the tower on that same night. When they had removed the stone from the hole the father entered with no suspicion of the trap stretched below. He quickly leaped to the pavement, just as he had done yesterday and the day before, and the poor fellow, clothed and booted, landed in the vat up to his chin. He was encompassed by the glue and could move neither hand nor foot, nor any other part of his body, except his tongue, which still remained free. With a groan the wretch called to his son and told him the trap which he had fallen into. He begged him quickly to cut off his head, before anyone else came, and get out of there. He did not want to be recognized and so bring eternal shame and disgrace to his family. The son tried to drag out his father with all his might. When he realized that he was struggling to no purpose, he began to be very doubtful which of two courses to follow. On the one hand, he was horrified to bloody his hands with the murder of his father, but on the other he feared he would be caught if his father were recognized. Love repelled him from the murder, fear and necessity demanded it. Then, not knowing what else to do, he cut off the head of his father with his knife and fled away with it.

Early in the morning of the next day the king rose from his bed and entered the tower. He ran to the vat, found the hole in the wall, and discovered that the surface of the asphalt was completely stained with blood. He had discovered his thief, but decapitated. Quickly he ran to his advisor, that same old man, and announced that the thief had been caught, but he was headless. When the old man heard this, he smiled a little and said, "I am amazed at the cunning of this robber. Because he was of noble birth he did not wish to betray himself or his family. Therefore he made his companion cut off his head. So now it seems to me that you will have difficulty in recovering your treasure or recognizing the thief."

The king strongly urged the old man to give him a plan, saying that he did not care so much about the lost treasure as in learning the identity of the thief.

The old man said to him, "Take the one you've caught out of the vat, have him tied to the tail of a powerful horse and dragged through the squares and streets of the cities of your kingdom. Then order armed knights to follow, and if they see any men or women weeping at the sight of the body, have them seized and brought before you. If a friend or a wife or his sons see him, they will have to weep."

The king believed the advice of the old man to be good. He quickly ordered the trunk to be tied by its feet to a powerful horse and dragged through the nearest city accompanied by armed knights. While the wretch was being dragged, he happened to pass the door of his own house. His elder son, who had been his partner in crime, was standing before the door. When he saw his father dragged so pitifully he did not dare to weep, but he was unable to restrain the tears. To provide an excuse he grabbed a piece of wood and while pretending to be cutting something purposely cut off the thumb of his left hand. Using this as a pretext he moaned and wept. His mother, brothers and sisters came and tore their clothes, faces and hair with their hands, mourning the wretchedness of the father under the guise of the son. The knights surrounded them, seized them, and took them to the king, who was overwhelmed with joy, hoping to recover what he had lost. He promised them their lives and his favor if they would confess the crime and return his treasure. In such a precarious situation, however, the young man put on a bold front. "O most glorious king," he said, "we were not weeping because we cared about that miserable trunk, but because this unfortunate day saw the loss of my left thumb. That is why we wept, tore our faces, and rent our hair; because today, alas, while still young, I have lost the use of this important part of the body."

The king believed that the stump, which was still flowing with blood, was sure proof of the truth and pitied the young man for his misfortune. "There is no wonder," he said, "if a man grieves when such a thing happens to him. Go in peace, and be wary of this ill-omened day in the future."

In this way he freed himself and his family by his cleverness and returned home. The king was fooled by the likeness of the truth and returned to the old man for further advice.

He insisted that the task was almost impossible, but suggested that the corpse be dragged again through the same city. This was done. When they came to the same house as before the son again could not bear the grief in his heart secretly and threw his own child into a well which was near the house. Then, ripping his face with his nails, he tearfully called for help to rescue his son. The mother came with her sons, they ran around the well, they wept, some climbed down the well on ropes to rescue the boy, others dragged them back again. But why go on? He was arrested and taken to the king a second time.

Meanwhile the corpse had been dragged through other cities to no purpose and was brought back to the king barely stuck together by a few bones and muscles.

When the king saw the same man, whom he had sent away before, brought before him a second time he was amazed. "You rogue," he said, "how can these tricks help you? The highest gods betray you, your thefts and crimes accuse you. Give me back my treasure and I swear by my power and the power of great Jupiter that I shall neither kill nor mutilate you but let you return sound, whole and free."

Then the robber used great craftiness. He sighed from the bottom of his heart and spoke in this way: "O! I am the unluckiest of men," he said, "whom the gods attack with such hatred. They let no day pass without inflicting upon me sorrow and suffering of body and soul. Yesterday unluckily saw the loss of my thumb; this day, even more unluckily, saw my only son drowned in the well. And now look! I am asked about the king's treasure." Then pouring out feigned tears (or rather very real ones) he said, "O King, you would do an outstanding act of kindness to a poor wretch if you took from him a life which seems more painful than every torture, every death."

When the king saw that the young man was overwhelmed with grief and sought death as a favor, and when he realized that he had truly lost his son that day and his thumb the day before, he pitied him and let him go. In addition he gave him a hundred marks of silver as consolation. So the king, once again deceived, returned to his advisor and said that the plan had not been successful.

Then the old man said to the king, "There is only one thing left to do to capture the surviving thief. If this is not successful, nothing else will be. Choose forty of your bravest knights. Let twenty of these have black armor and black horses, and let the other twenty have white horses and white armor. Hang the body by its feet from a tree and let them guard it night and day, the twenty white knights arranged around it on one side, the twenty black knights on the other. If they guard it vigilantly they will catch your thief. He will not permit his companion to hang there too long, even if he knows that he will suffer immediate death."

The king did as the old man had instructed. He arrayed his knights in black and white armor around the suspended corpse. The thief was indeed unable to bear the insult to him and to his father and preferred to die once than to live a long life of shame. He resolved to rescue his father's body from this foul mockery or die there with him. Cunningly he made a suit of divided armor, one side white, the other side black. Armed in this he mounted a horse which had white trapping on one side and black trapping on the other. Then by the light of the moon he passed through the midst of the knights, so that the black side of his armor fooled the twenty white knights, and the white side fooled the blacks. The black knights thought he was one of the whites, and the whites thought he was one of the blacks. He passed through them, went to his father, and took him down from the tree. When morning came the knights saw that the robber's body had been stolen. In consternation they returned to the king and told him how the knight had fooled them with his black and white armor. At this point the king lost all hope of success and stopped searching for the thief and his treasure.

"You see, O King, how many times that king was deceived, and in what ways. The world has been muffled with such shadows of ignorance that often what is most unjust and false is judged by men to be the most just and true. Do not kill your son too quickly. Perhaps some truth lies hidden which will enable you to free yourself from shame and your son from death. In return for the example which I have given, I ask you to let your son live today. Tomorrow, unless a better fortune intervenes, you can do what you have postponed."

"O venerable wise man," said the king, "you would certainly have been enriched by me if you had asked for great honors. Since you have only asked the life of my son for one day, I think it wrong to deny you." Then the king with his son and all who were there returned home and the wise man said farewell to the king and departed.

On the next day, since no compassionate law had been found to intercede on behalf of Lucinius, the kings and their nobles and all the people again gathered on the same plain. The fire blazed strongly, and the father ordered his son to be thrown into the flames. The friends of the king were sad and disheartened. On the other hand, the queen and her sympathizers rejoiced. In addition they began to accuse the king of cowardice and weakness. While they were torn with different emotions, suddenly an old man of reverend aspect riding on a black horse came through the multitude straight to the king. In his right hand he carried a branch of living olive as a sign of peace. After he had greeted the king and those with him he inquired the reason for the spectacle to which so many people had come. The king replied that his only son was the reason for the spectacle and he told the crime and the sentence of the nobles. Then he asked the old man who he was, where he came from and what news he brought.

"I," he said, "am a Roman citizen, and I am called one of the seven wise men. It is my custom to offer from the treasury of my heart new things and old things to the kings and nobles of the world. Since chance has led me here, if you will permit I shall also give you an example. An old one, indeed, but perhaps new to you."

The king signalled for silence with his hand and quickly quelled the tumult of the people. The wise man, standing on a hill, began.

The Story of the Third Wise Man

The Old Man

Once when the Roman republic was very new and governed by its early kings, a certain king died and left the throne to his son, who was still a young man. As usually happens during a change of rulers, war broke out and the city itself was besieged by its enemies. After the siege had lasted many months the citizens began to die of hunger. Every day battles were fought outside the walls; inside fear and hunger weighed upon the people. The young king, advised by his nobles, who were as young as he, decreed that all the old men and women in the city be killed. He said that those who could not bear arms, who could not feed themselves by their own labor, were worthy to die, since they ate as much as stronger men. Those who protected their parents were also sentenced to death. Parents, therefore, were slaughtered by their sons without mercy, and (horrible to say) a father had no enemy more savage than his own son. The cruelty was so widespread that in the entire city no old person escaped death, with the exception of one wise old man who was hidden in a deep cave by his son. The only other person who knew about it was the son's wife, who was sworn to secrecy. Everyone in whom the light of wisdom gleamed like a ray of the sun was killed.

Not much later a treaty of peace was made with the enemy and the siege was lifted. The young king had no wise man and no counselor who had knowledge of the law and justice. There were many instigators of evil, however, men of his own age who dragged him down to their level of impiety and wickedness. He became corrupt, allowed emotion to replace reason, enslaved his subjects, plotted against his friends, and thought he could do anything he desired. The old laws had perished and were no longer used. The impious evil men usually defeated the cause of the just, and the innocent were punished unjustly. Good morals were corrupted and vices flourished in place of virtues. If this disordered city with its dominions could have spoken about its government and its rulers, it would sorrowfully have had to say what a wise man once said: "Woe to the land whose king is a boy and whose nobles carouse till morning."[37]

Meanwhile, however, the young man who had saved his father's life remained at court, since he was of the nobility. When trials were held there he told them to his father in the cave, who would give him the proper solution. When he returned to court he would try them carefully and come to the proper decision. Day by day he increased in wisdom and gradually led the king to an upright and honorable life. He and the king became so friendly that he was soon appointed the first noble and counselor of the kingdom, even above those who were more noble and more wealthy.

When the other young nobles realized that he was raised above them and they were no longer of importance but were pushed aside, they considered how they might bring him to trial. Their hatred grew and they plotted against him. As he continued to increase in virtue and they in villainy, they began to suspect that the father of the youth might be alive and teaching his son wisdom. Although they often whispered the truth among themselves, they did not dare to speak openly, but planned a trick to betray the father and accuse the son. They went to the king and asked him to decree a holiday during which games and festivities were to be held. In addition they asked that each one be ordered to bring with him his best friend, his worst enemy, a good actor, and a faithful slave. The king agreed, the holiday was established, the nobles were summoned, and all attended. One man brought his father as his best friend, another his wife, another his mistress with his bitterest enemy and a slave whom he had found faithful. Each one with great arrogance brought with him an actor whom he believed to be good.

Meanwhile the young man had gone to his father and told him what was going on. He soon recognized the deception and asked his son if he had made any enemies. When he learned that he had earned the jealousy and hatred of all his friends, he said, "My son, I know that this festival which has been decreed concerns you and me. When you bring me before the king as your best friend, you will immediately be accused of despising the king's command because you did not kill me. But you must act differently than your enemies desire. Forget about me for the present. Instead, after all the others have entered, bring to the king a dog, an ass, your wife, and your little son." Then his father instructed him which of these he should call his friend, which his enemy, which his slave, which his actor, and how he should explain his choice.

After all the nobles had gathered and shown the king what they had brought, the young man entered with his group, quite different from the others, and stood before the king. All the hall was echoing to the sound of the musicians' instruments, and when the ass, a stupid animal, heard the noise it lifted its ears, stretched out its tail, and brayed so loudly that it shook the whole palace and attracted the attention of the king and all present. His enemies, who realized they had failed, began to mock him and said ironically to the king that he certainly had a wise and good counselor who would fill the palace with such monstrosities. The king, however, paid no attention to the words of the slanderers (he knew this was not done without a reason) but asked the young man what each thing he had brought symbolized. He answered him point by point.

"My dog symbolizes my best friend," replied the young man. "He goes with me wherever I go and does not fear to endure the danger of rivers, the knives of bandits, and the teeth of wild beasts. He even despises death for my sake. Often he returns from hunting with noble spoils of the chase for me and my guests; never happy without me, never sorrowful with me. Certainly, O King, I could never find another friend so pure and faithful. I think not even you could be such.

"I have brought my ass as my most faithful and patient slave. Every morning he goes to the forest and returns burdened with logs. When he puts these aside, he carries the grain to the mill and brings it back when it is ground. Then he takes water bags to the fountain and returns home when they are full. He does this daily without a murmur, without hesitation, and does not request fine clothes and rich food. A little bit of straw or hay is enough for him after his daily tasks. O King, where else can I find such a slave? Nowhere, certainly.

"Where can I find a better actor than my little son? Every day he puts on new shows. When he tries to imitate what he sees or hears, he uses comic gestures. He stammers words which he cannot handle properly, and when he cannot say at all what he is thinking he illustrates it by signs and motions of the body. One moment he is gay, the next moment he is sad. He cries and laughs, not deliberately as other actors do, but simply as nature and his youth compel. For all this he asks no reward.

"Finally, I have brought my wife as my worst enemy."

When his wife realized that she had been saved last for this insult, and recalled her faith, pity, and kindness toward her husband and his father, she blazed with fury and hardly permitted him to finish his words before she said, "O you most depraved and thankless man! He has forgotten the kindness and the pity I showed to his father for many years in the cave where he was hidden to save his life. How dare he call me an enemy in the presence of the king and the people?"

"You see," said the young man, "I was right, O King. My wife is just what I said. For only a word she has betrayed my hidden father and condemned me to death."

In this way a very wise man once instructed his son to beware of the wife of his bosom, desiring to show that she was a false friend. When enemies are known it is easy to beware of them, but no one can avoid a wife (or a hypocritical enemy) who always oppresses us because she pretends excessive love on the surface but contrives treachery in her heart. The king was amazed at the cleverness of the youth. He realized the truth of his words and thwarted his accusers. "Go without fear," he said, "and if your father is alive do not keep him from our festival."

The old man was led from the cave and because of his great wisdom he was appointed father of the city and judge of its fatherland

by the king. In a short time he restored justice and the laws to their
old position. He ripped away base habits, he implanted good ones, he
restored peace, and when he died he left many who followed his
virtuous ways.

"Now I have finished my example and I must go. I ask nothing
from you except that you grant your son one more day of life, since I
know that there is hidden evidence. If you find this it will free you
from murder and your son from punishment." The king granted the
wise man the life of his son. They said farewell and the king returned
to the palace with his retinue.

Again throughout the day and night consultations were held by the
nobles. The laws were considered anew, but the only punishment
found was burning alive. In the morning the king with all his
company followed his son to the place of punishment. Again he was
stripped, his hands bound behind his back, and he was ordered to be
thrown into the fire, which was burning fiercely. Suddenly a very old
man in a Roman toga sitting on a morello mule appeared before King
Dolopathos. All wondered who he was. When he had properly
greeted the king and those with him, he asked who that handsome
young man was, what his crime, and how he deserved to become a
spectacle for so many people and food for such a fire. At the words of
the old man, the father was gripped with sorrow for his son, but with
a kingly sense of justice and fairness he repressed his grief. "O
reverend old man," he replied, "that is my son who returned ten days
ago from his studies. Somehow he became mute. The queen received
him into her bedchamber and promised to restore his speech. She
then revealed him to us as an adulterer, the invader of his father's bed,
even though mute. For so great a crime he was given such a sentence
by our kings and nobles. But since fortune has brought you here,
please tell me your race and country and what you think about this."

"As you can tell from my clothing," he said, "I am a Roman citizen,
and I am called one of the seven wise men. For forty years now I
have travelled the world studying the justice, the laws, the customs,
and the vicissitudes of men, and I have never seen anything as amazing as this. A father has condemned his only son to the deadly flames!
I shall tell you what I think about this. I think your nobels inter-

preted the laws wrongly. They have been too concerned about the punishment and death of your son and not concerned enough about his life. I believe you will understand this better if I use an example and tell you what happened once. It is my solemn duty to give such gifts to kings and nobles." The king with great eagerness awaited the example of the wise man and commanded silence. The wise man in moderate tones began.

The Story of the Fourth Wise Man

The Creditor

There was once a certain powerful nobleman who had a strong castle and many other possessions. After his wife died his only heir was a daughter whom he decided to educate in the liberal arts, thinking that training in the arts and the books of the philosophers would give her the wisdom (which is better than strength) to protect her inheritance. A woman is physically weak and unable to bear arms. Nor was he wrong. She obtained such knowledge and cleverness from her studies that she even learned the art of magic without a teacher. Sometime after this her father took to his bed with a high fever. He realized that he could not recover and made a will in which he left everything to his daughter. When his affairs were in order he died. The girl, now mistress of the inheritance, decided that she would marry no man except one equal to her in wisdom and noble birth. Many young noblemen, attracted by her beauty or wealth, came to seek her hand in marriage. They wooed her with prayers, enticed her with gifts, gave much and promised more. She, however, wisely spurned and scorned no one, but offered to marry anyone on one condition. The suitor had to pay her a hundred marks of silver on the first night and then might enjoy her and her charms. On the next morning, if they were both satisfied with the deed, they would hold a proper marriage in public. When this condition was made known many youths and many men of more advanced age came to offer her the twenty pounds of marks, but they always returned without enjoying her embraces and without their money. With her magic art she had cast a spell upon the feather of a night owl, and when she put this under the head of the one lying with her he immediately fell into a deep sleep and did not move until the dawn of the next day, or until she removed the feather. In this way she stripped many men of their money and stored up great treasure for herself, increasing her fortune by others' losses.

Among those who poured money down this bottomless pit was a certain noble youth sufficient in nobility of birth but poor. Finding the hundred marks beyond his means, he borrowed the money and accepted the maid's condition. When she had received the money she spent the day feasting and drinking a great deal with the youth. At night both of them lay naked together on the soft bed covering, but first she placed the owl's feather under the youth's pillow. He had not even found a comfortable place in the bed when he fell asleep and forgot the maiden beside him. At dawn she arose and took away the feather. When he awoke, terribly upset, she sent him about his own business.

The young man, however, angry that he had been fooled, asked a certain rich serf to lend him another hundred marks of silver, since he wished either to lose the money again or take the girl's virginity. Now once in a fit of rage the young man had cut off the serf's foot, and with this in mind the serf promised him the money on the condition that he must repay it within a year. If he failed to repay, the serf could cut from the flesh and bones of the youth a weight equal to a hundred marks. The youth carelessly agreed, and in addition he gave him a contract sealed and signed in his own handwriting.

When he had received the money, he returned to the girl and offered it to her. She accepted and they spent the day happily until evening. Later, when the bedroom had been made ready and the feather placed under the pillow as usual, the girl sent him in first. As he approached the bed where he had lain before, the thought occurred to him that the stupor had come upon him because the bed was soft and comfortable. He picked up the pillow and removed it. By a lucky chance this dislodged the owl's feather. Then he lay down on the bed, kept his eyes open, and fought sleep with all his strength. She believed that the youth had fallen asleep again because of her magic and carelessly lay naked next to him. After he had pretended he was sleeping heavily for a little while, he drew the maiden to him and demanded his due. Confused and astonished, she had to fulfill her promise. But why go on? The whole night was spent in pleasure. In the morning both were in complete agreement and they were properly married before their friends and relatives, although many were surprised and even envious.

In these happy circumstances, the young man forgot his creditor and did not repay the money within the allotted time. The cripple was overjoyed at the chance to gain vengeance for his injury and went to the king who was then ruling the country. He brought a complaint against the young man, showed the handwriting as witness of the agreement, and demanded that justice be done. The king was horrified at the cruel contract; nevertheless, because he was a very just man, he ordered the youth to come to reply to his accuser's complaints. Only then did he remember the debt. Terrified by the king's authority he went with a group of his friends, taking a great amount of gold and silver to the court. His enemy showed him the handwriting, which he admitted to be his, and the king ordered his nobles to pass sentence. They decreed that the cripple could do what the contract stipulated or instead he could receive as much money as he wished in payment. The king then asked the cripple if he would take double the amount and spare the youth. He refused and the king spent many days trying to convince him.

One day the wife of the young man, in men's clothing, dismounted from her horse before the palace of the king. She had changed her features and voice by her magic power. She approached the king and greeted him reverently. When asked who she was and where she came from, she replied that she was a knight who had come from the farthest parts of the world and was an expert interpreter of justice, the laws and trials. The king was overjoyed and ordered her (whom he thought to be a knight) to sit in judgment and conclude the case between the cripple and the young man. When both parties were summoned she said, "Cripple, according to the sentence of the king and the nobles you are permitted to carve from the flesh of the young man a weight equivalent to a hundred marks. But what will you gain except possibly death if you kill him? It is better that you receive your money seven times or even ten times over."

He said that he would not accept even ten thousand marks. Then she ordered a gleaming white cloth to be stretched on the floor and the youth, naked and bound, laid on it. When this was done she said to the cripple, "Cut off a weight of flesh equivalent to your marks with any instrument you wish. But if you cut away a needle's point more or less than the just weight or if one drop of blood stains the cloth, since blood is the substance of the young man, you will immediately die a thousand deaths. You will be torn into a thousand pieces and thrown to the beasts and the birds, your whole family will undergo the same punishment, and your estate will be confiscated."

He began to quake at this horrible sentence and said, "There is no man, only God, who could control his hand so as to take neither more nor less. I shall not take the chance. I free the youth, I dismiss the debt, and I shall give him a thousand marks for reconciliation."

So the youth was freed by the wisdom of his wife and joyfully went his way. Who could believe that the youth would be freed by this subtlety, O King? You see that life and death, freedom and condemnation, differed by only a needle's point. I wish you to be guided by this example and ask you, for my sake, or rather out of the goodness of your heart, to let your son live until tomorrow. Meanwhile read the Roman laws again. You will surely find that they contain salvation for your son along with condemnation.

All this time the king had listened intently to the words of the wise man. "Since," he said, "you have told me an amazingly subtle example, I think it is right and just to grant your request, out of regard for you and my own good." The wise man was dismissed, and the king again returned to the palace with his son and the people who were present.

The conscience of the queen and her supporters in wickedness was seared as if by a branding iron. They were tortured by grief and fear lest the evil which they plotted against the innocent fall upon their own heads. No longer did the queen eat or sleep with the king. Like a beast thirsting for human blood she furiously scorned the darts and javelins with which the wise men obscurely pricked her every day. Raging and scorning the king himself, she abused and insulted him. She shouted that a man who permitted a shameless youth to live so long was slothful, unjust, and unworthy of the name and honor of a king. The king, however, ignoring all this, ordered the laws to be studied again, but his hopes and desires were frustrated.

Once more, therefore, all the multitude of kings and nobles, men and women, with the father and the son, gathered at the place of punishment. Again the fire burned fiercely, the flames spread in every direction. It was a terrible sight to behold. Amid all this, however, the conduct of the young Lucinius was outstanding. When he saw some weeping, some mocking, the flames rising to the sky, he neither broke his imposed silence nor changed color. He always remained the same, without a word, without hesitation, as a tame animal awaits without fear the altar prepared for it. His father was hurrying to deliver him to the flames when suddenly an old man like the others in every respect—dress, features, and age—dismounted from a horse on which he rode. He greeted the king and those around him and asked what crime had been committed worthy of such punishment. The king told, in order, what had happened to his son and the sentence of the nobles. Then he asked the old man where he came from.

"I am a Roman citizen," he answered, "and I am called one of the seven wise men. It is my custom to wander through many foreign lands. I give to kings and nobles different examples and I speak of the vicissitudes of mortals. But to come to the present, I find it astounding that your son could or would even wish to commit such impiety when he was grieving for his dead mother and his loss of speech. It does not seem logical to me that anyone, especially a philosopher, who always desires virtue, could possibly wish to descend to such lust after such terrible misfortunes occuring at almost the same time, so to speak. Since this must seem doubtful to all, or rather contrary to the truth, let me give you, O King, some useful advice. Then you may imitate the deed of a certain just king and spare your son. But whatever you are going to do about this, listen to a thing which happened." Then the king commanded all to be silent under penalty of death, and the wise man began his tale.

The Story of the Fifth Wise Man

The Son of the Widow

Once a certain king of the Romans marched out with his army against the enemy, who had seized a great part of his kingdom. He happened to pass through a certain little village where a poor widow with her only son lived in a little house. Her only possession in the entire world was a little chicken. When the army passed before her house, the son of the king, a very young man, cast the hawk which he bore on his arm (as nobles do) against the chicken of the widow. While the hawk was strangling the poor chicken with its hooked talons, the widow's son ran up to help the little bird, struck the hawk with a club, and killed it. The son of the king became very angry over this, and to avenge his hawk stabbed the son of the widow with a dagger and then went away. What could the poor widow do? She had been deprived of her only son and the little that she owned. She quickly ran after the king and with tears, words, and groans demanded that he avenge her son, who had been unjustly killed. The king was a merciful man and pitied her condition. He stopped and gently and kindly advised the widow to await his return from the enemy. "Then I shall avenge your son as you wish," he said.

"But what will happen if you are killed in the war?" the widow asked. "Who will avenge my son?"

"I shall order my successor to act in my place," he replied.

"But what credit will you receive if another avenges a man killed while you were alive and ruling?" she asked.

"I shall receive none," he said.

"Do not leave it to another," said the widow. "If you act now you will obtain praise from men and reward from the gods."

Moved as much by the reasoning of the widow as by pity, the king postponed the war and returned to the city. When he learned that his own son was the killer of the widow's son, he said, "I think your chicken has been repaid by the death of the hawk. For your dead son, I give you two choices. If you wish I shall kill my son, or if you decide that it is better for him to live, I shall give him to you in place of the dead one. He will love you as a mother, respect you as a queen, fear you as a mistress and serve you all the days of your life."

She decided it would be better for her if the son of the king lived than died. She chose him in place of her dead son, was taken from her hut to the palace, and exchanged her rags and tatters for garments dyed with purple. After this the king set out to fight the enemy.

"Consider this, O King, and emulate the deed of a most just and pious king. Consider how he displayed unbending justice and yet saved his son by his wisdom. By this act he avenged not his own wrong but that of another, not the wrong of some powerful person but that of a poor little widow. Because of this example, spare your son, even if he wished to commit incest (although this seems incredible to me). Satisfy the queen and her attendants as they wish. But if you are unwilling to change the sentence of your nobles, let me prevail upon you to grant him an extra day. Tomorrow, as even today, you will easily find logs and fire to burn your son."

"O wisest of men," the king said, "you offer me good advice, but since I cannot do what you advise at least I shall grant this last request."

The wise man was dismissed. The king, with those who had met there, and the queen and her attendants, raging like wild beasts, returned to the palace.

In the morning the crowd of kings and nobles and people went, as before, to the place of punishment. The fire was blazing as before and Lucinius was ordered thrown in to be burnt. But no one dared to fulfill the order of the king. Suddenly a certain old man with venerable white hair in a Roman toga made his way slowly through the crowd of men and women. With amazement they watched him approach and greet the king and those around him. He said that he wished to learn why such a multitude of people had gathered there. The king told him everything which had happened to his son and the sentence passed upon him. Then he asked the old man who he was, where he came from, and the reason of his coming.

He replied, "I am called one of the seven wise men, and as my clothing indicates I was born in the city of Rome, mistress of the world. Nothing but chance has brought me to you. From my youth I have been accustomed to wander the length and breadth of the world meeting kings and nobles. Although I am believed to be one of the seven wisest men, yet I always find something to learn as well as teach. But to speak about the present, as I can foresee from the logical consequences of your words that I may speak without insulting you or your friends, it seems to me to be neither true nor similar to the truth but rather absolutely illogical to think that your son could even have dreamed of this crime, much less have wished to do it. How could such lust follow such sorrow in such a moment of time, so to speak? Indeed, pain, grief, and sadness are wont to arise from sorrow, and lust from pleasure. Grief and joy, sadness and laughter, lust and philosophy are contraries and repel each other. A philosopher who loves virtue and opposes vices cannot yield to lust, which is the vice directly opposed to philosophy. Otherwise he would not be a philosopher. Therefore it seems to me, if I may speak a little boldly, that someone has falsely accused your son out of hatred or jealousy and that you and your nobles, if I may say it with all due respect, have been deluded by a verisimilitude. Nor do I wonder that the wisdom of good men could be betrayed, since at times even the iniquity of evil men lies to itself and the malice of the perverse is deluded. But hear the following example which will make this more obvious."

At the order of the king all grew silent, and the wise man began.

Story of the Sixth Wise Man

The Sons of the Bandit

A certain famous bandit, who wished to gain riches by thievery, robbery and murder, gathered a gang of men eager for a base and depraved way of life. He was made their chief and placed his headquarters not in fortified cities or armed camps, but in the wilderness, living in deep, rocky caverns and the obscure hiding places of the forests. Day and night without fail he and his band hid at the more difficult crossings of the king's highways and ambushed the travelers. Whomever ill luck brought to him, of whatever condition or sex, he robbed and murdered without mercy. He lived this evil life until he was an old man and had acquired great piles of gold and silver, and become wealthy. Knowing, however, that nothing goes unpunished, that every secret is revealed, and that a great sinner cannot revel too long in iniquity,[38] he renounced his depraved habits, although it was rather late, and spent the rest of his life practicing honor and virtue.

All were amazed that an Ethiopian had suddenly changed his skin and the leopard his spots.

Finally, when he was very old, he decided to educate his three sons in pursuits more honorable than his own had been, and he suggested to them many different ways of life. Each one was permitted to choose whatever he wished and be supported by his father with a third of his estate. When they had consulted with each other they all decided that they preferred no other pursuit than that which their father had practiced for so long. When he heard this, their father replied to them, "Since you have all turned away from honor and the straight path to the crooked road which leads to death, a road paved with danger from which there is usually no return, I hope you enjoy your decision. You are seeking riches for yourselves by robbery and a life of danger. You will be burnt by the sun in summer and frozen in winter. Not one of you will ever have a penny of my wealth. Know that fortune permits few followers of this kind of life to come to a happy end."

They despised their father's advice and the next night they stole the queen's horse, an animal beyond price, in this way: they collected a pile of plants which we call vetch (they had heard that the horse's appetite was such that he would eat no other food except this herb) and carefully hid the younger brother in the pile. Around evening they took it to the market place as if to sell it. The horse's guard was walking there as he usually did and happened to see the bundle. Since he had no knowledge of the plot, he bought the vetch, put it on his shoulders, and carried it to the stable. He gave it to the horse and, after re-barring the door, went to sleep. Around midnight, when all mortals sleep the heaviest, the robber got up like a "snake hidden in the green grass,"[39] put golden reins on the horse, covered it with silk, put on the saddle, and adjusted the bridle. All these things had golden decorations and the metal tinkled, so he covered them with wax to muffle the sound. When this was done he opened the door, mounted the horse, and galloped at full speed to the place set by the brothers.

But their attempt at banditry did not turn out well, since he was seen by the city guards. As he was fleeing speedily from them he came to the appointed place, they were all caught, and the next morning taken before the queen. When she saw that they were handsome men and heard that they were the sons of that once-famous bandit (he was a friend of the queen's) she locked them in prison and ordered their father's presence. On his arrival the queen asked him if he wished to ransom his sons. He refused to pay even a penny for them. "All right," said the queen, "tell me the worst misfortunes or dangers which ever happened to you while you were a bandit, and I shall set your sons free."

He (I cannot do better than use his own words) said, "According to the poet 'The loss of a word is a little loss'[40] and in this case my words can save me money. Remember your promise," he said to the queen, "and listen to one of the worst things that ever happened to me."

Polyphemus

Once we heard that a giant, who possessed much gold and silver, was living in the wilderness about twenty miles from civilization. We collected a band of a hundred robbers greedy for gold and came with great difficulty to his dwelling. He wasn't there and we were pleased to take all the gold and silver we could find. But when we were carelessly returning, that giant and nine others unexpectedly came upon us. We were captured—it's a disgrace—a hundred captured by ten!

They divided us up, and I with nine others unfortunately came into the possession of the one we had robbed. That colossus of a man, more than thirteen cubits tall, tied our hands behind our backs and herded us to his cave like ten little sheep. When we offered him a lot of money for ransom he replied that he would take nothing else but our flesh and leaping among us seized the fattest one and killed him. Then tearing him limb from limb he threw him into a pot and cooked him. But why go on? He wasn't the only one! He cooked and ate all the others until I was the only one left. And ugh! he even forced me to help him eat the others. When he was going to slaughter me I lied and said I was a doctor and told him I could cure a painful eye disease which he had, if he would let me live. He gladly granted me this request if I would heal his eyes and asked me to hurry and prepare the medicine. I put a pint of oil on the fire and mixed in a great amount of chalk, salt, sulphur, arsenic, and other things which I knew to be very harmful for the eyes. From this I made a paste. As it was boiling on the fire, I unexpectedly tipped it over the head of my patient. The boiling oil ran over all the parts of his body and burned off the skin, his body wrinkled up, and his muscles stiffened. He lost what little sight he had left. You should have seen that giant colossus rolling on the floor like an epileptic, roaring like a lion, bellowing like a bull, a horrible sight to see.

After he had rolled around for a long time and could not lessen the pain he madly seized his club and tried to find me with it. He struck the walls and the floor like a battering ram. What could I do? Where could I run? There was no window in the house and the only exit was the door, and that was fastened with iron bars. While he was running around searching all the corners of the house, I could do nothing else except climb to the roof by a ladder, grab a beam, and hang there by my hands all day and night. But when my strength gave out I had to climb down again and sometimes hide behind the legs of the giant, sometimes among his flock of sheep.

He had about a thousand sheep, which he counted every day. When he sent them to pasture he always kept a fat one for himself to eat. Somehow or other (maybe by black magic) they always returned from pasture of their own free will without the loss of a single one, and he would let them in. One day when he was sending them out and counting them, I decided to escape and put the shaggy skin of a ram around my shoulders, fitted horns on my head, and mixed with the flock. I advanced to be counted. When he touched me he felt that I was fat and held me back. "Today," he said, "I shall stuff my empty belly with you." Seven times I tried to escape, and seven times he held me back. Each time I slipped out of his hands. When he felt me one more time, he suddenly became very angry and threw me out the door. "Go on!" he said, "let the wolves eat you. That will teach you to slip away from me so often."

I was tossed a stone's throw from the door and I began to mock him because I had deceived him so many times and escaped. He took a gold ring from his finger, stretched it out to me, and said, "Take this as a gift. It is not proper that you leave such a great man as I without a present."

I put it on my finger and immediately, afflicted by some curse, I was forced to go around shouting, "Here I am! Here I am!"

Like a mighty mountain he followed my shouts without wavering, although blind, leaping over the smaller trees and sometimes knocking them down when his legs struck them. When he was near me and I could neither stop shouting nor take off the ring, I had to bite off my finger and throw it and the ring at him. I lost my finger but saved my life.

When the bandit had told this story, he said to the queen, "Well, I have told you about many dangers which happened to me in one adventure for the ransom of my son. I'll also add some other experiences for the other two."

The Witches

When I escaped from the giant I began to wander through the solitude of a vast wasteland. I did not know where I was going. I often climbed lofty firs and tall cedars and mountain ridges in an attempt to see from their tops how far I was from civilization. Nothing met my eye except forest and sky everywhere.[41] I descended from mountain tops to valleys deep as an abyss and I climbed from them to mountains high as the sky. I shudder to remember how many lions, bears, boars, leopards, and wolves I met; how many herds of gazelles and wild asses; how many satyrs and other monsters snarling out something barbarous at me; how many serpents, with two heads and even three, hissing at my sight.

When I had wandered two days through the steep mountains and vaulted valleys, past wild beasts and serpents, I came at last, hungry, tired, and frightened, to the peak of a certain mountain as the sun was setting westward. Turning my eyes to a certain valley, gloomy and fearful because of its depth, I suddenly noticed far away some smoke rising as if from an oven. Marking the place, I quickly descended. Then at the foot of the mountain I came upon three bandits who had just been hanged. At this I shuddered with awful terror and began to falter and lose hope, thinking that I had chanced upon the dwelling of some giant. But we become bold when necessary. Although I was tired of living I went on and on until I saw a hut with the door open.

Looking inside I found a poor woman with a little boy sitting at the hearth. I entered and approached her. When I had greeted her I asked her what she was doing there alone, if she had a husband, and how far I was from human society. She said I was thirty miles from civilization. Then she added tearfully that last night she and her son had been stolen from her husband's side by those who are called witches and brought to this wilderness. They had ordered her to cook her son and later to serve him up to be eaten. When I heard this I pitied her misfortune and promised to free the both of them.

Although I was very tired and very hungry, although I had lost hope of living, nevertheless I hastened back to those three bandits whom I had seen hanging there, cut down the middle one, who was the fattest, and brought him to the woman. I advised her to entrust her son to me, cook the bandit and serve him to the witches. She agreed and let me have her son. Then she cut the bandit into pieces and put him over the fire. I hid the little boy well in a hollow tree and concealed myself near the house, wishing to see the monsters when they arrived and to help the woman if necessary.

Suddenly, just as the sun was dyeing the western waves, I saw descending from the mountains what appeared to be thousands of apes. They came with a great clattering, dragging something bloody behind them. When they entered the house they built a great pyre and ate the bloody thing, tearing it with their teeth. After a time they took the accursed pot from the fire and dividing the pieces of the cooked bandit among themselves re-enacted the banquet of Thyestes.[42] When this was done the one who seemed to be their leader asked the woman whether they had eaten her son or another. When she answered that it had been her son, the witch said, "O no, I believe you saved your son and served us one of the three bandits. I can prove it quickly. Go," she said to three other witches, "and bring me back a piece of flesh from each one of the bandits."

When I heard this I ran and hung myself by my hands between the two bandits. The witches arrived and cut two pieces from the buttocks of the bandits and a third piece from my thigh. I still have a deep scar there to prove it. Then they returned to their leader.

When he had told this much of the tale, the bandit said to the queen, "I think that this part of the dangerous adventure should be enough ransom for my second son. I shall continue on behalf of the third."

Seriously wounded, I climbed down from the tree on which I was hanging and bound up the wound with linen cloth. Although I tried, I could not stop the blood which flowed like a river to the ground. I returned to my hiding place more concerned about the safety of the woman, whom I had promised to defend, than about myself. There I often fainted because of the great loss of blood, hunger, lack of sleep and weariness. The leader of the witches was tasting the pieces of the bandits. When she had tried my flesh she said with her bloody mouth, "Go and bring me the bandit in the middle. His flesh is fresher and tastes best."

At this I returned to the place and hung myself again between the bandits. The servants of darkness came again, took me down from the tree, and dragged me to the house by the hands and feet and hair over briers and rocks. They were all sharpening their teeth over me and their greedy mouths were gaping to devour me when suddenly with a great cry they fled like a storm through the door, the roof, and the cracks in the wall, and left me unharmed with the woman. They must have been terrified by some secret power opposed to them. After two or three hours the gleaming dawn put to flight the shadows of night and all the servants of darkness. I and the woman and the little boy with great difficulty came out of the wilderness after forty days and returned to civilization.[43] We had had nothing to eat but the roots of plants and the leaves of trees. Thus I restored her and her child to their family."

When he had finished his tale the bandit was happy to receive from the queen his three sons and many gifts.

"Consider then, O King, how those three brothers were deceived by their wicked nature. Consider how often their father deceived the giant Polyphemus and how he himself was deceived by the ring. Consider also how he deluded the witches of the night and how often. The inventors of evil are more often themselves betrayed. I have told you these things that you may realize that you and your nobles may also be easily deluded by a likeness to the truth, although you are good men. Avoid the pain of discovering sometime that your goodness had been deceived and accept my advice. Grant my request and allow your son to live."

The king answered the wise man, "Your advice and request show you to be good and merciful, O wise man, but I do not dare to yield completely, lest I seem to oppose the sentence of the nobles, as if it were unjust. Nor do I want them to think that I have accused the queen of false charges more on suspicion than truth. Today is the sixth day in which I have come here, and every day I am amazed to find that one of the seven wise men has chanced to be here. He gives me an example, he preserves my son's life, and sends me back to the laws, saying that there I shall find a way to free my son. I grant their requests, I postpone the sentence until tomorrow. I read the laws again, I consider every word, I weigh every syllable, but I cannot find what they promise. Because of this the kings and nobles and the queen are justly angry with me, the nobles because I seem not to trust their sentence, the queen because I postpone avenging her wrong. And so I am called soft, weak-minded, lukewarm, and unworthy of the name of king."

"Indeed," said the wise man, "since so far what I am asking has not been refused by any of the nobles, you would insult me unbearably if you refused me what you granted to others."

When the king heard this he said, "All right, I shall do what you ask, whatever happens." He returned to the palace with his retinue, and the wise man resumed his travels.

This time the kings and nobles were troubled that the king kept them so long at court. They went and threw themselves at his feet and beseeched him to pardon his son and give them permission to return home. They said that nothing could diminish his kingly power and glory and since the laws were human, not divine, he could interpret them from the point of view of mercy and kindness. On the other hand the queen, more savage than a tiger, and her company of poisonous snakes cried that the nobles' advice was wrong and their judgment corrupt. They said that the king was unjust and that the nobles were treacherous and had been bribed. Formerly they had passed a just sentence against the wicked youth, and now, abandoning justice, they were trying to free the one whom they had condemned.

King Dolopathos could not bear this wrangling. He swore by the gods that on that day he would put an end to their insults and their charge. He ordered the herald to proclaim throughout the city that all, from the lowest to the greatest, kings and nobles, slave and free, handmaid and matron, should assemble laden with logs at the place of punishment. When they had all hastened there as ordered, for the seventh time a raging fire was kindled, fiercer than usual. The king ordered his son thrown into the flames, but no one dared to lay a hand upon him.

Suddenly, to the amazement of all, an old man who far excelled the others in his outstanding appearance and the glory of his face and bearing descended from a chariot he was driving and greeted the king and those with him. His head was crowned with green ivy, and in his hand he bore a golden sceptre. Looking at the naked youth and the terrible flames he asked what awful crime he had committed to be made such an awful spectacle before the people. The king said that he was his son and added the facts about the return from his studies, how he had become mute and been entrusted to the queen, what she had accused him of, and the sentence passed by his kings and nobles.

The old man, showing his astonishment by his change of expression, said, "What man of sound mind could believe that a guileless youth of such noble appearance, and also a philosopher, could even think of such a crime, when he was involved in such sorrow? Has it not occurred to you that the queen and her wanton attendants were allured by his beauty and brought a false charge against him because he would not yield to their lust? Indeed, O King, you must remember the old proverb to trust a woman no more than a scorpion, and this especially applies to the one who sleeps in your bosom. But lest you think me foolish and thoughtless because I dare to say this, know that I am a Roman citizen and one of the seven wise men. It is proper that you hear from me how once the evil deed of a woman was exposed. It is not a long tale. Curb the noise of the turbulent people and listen for a little while."

The noise was checked by the order of the king, and the wise man began.

The Story of the Seventh Wise Man

The Swans

A certain young man, great according to those who judge greatness by noble birth and wealth, once went into the forest with his dogs to hunt. There he saw on a hill a stag whiter than snow, which had ten points on each horn. When it fled he galloped after it through the dark forest until he came to a deep valley thick with trees. The stag and his dogs disappeared, and he wandered in the valley blowing his horn and calling the dogs until he came upon a fountain in which a naked nymph was bathing. In one hand she held a golden necklace. At the sight of her beauty he fell deeply in love, quickly approached her, who was unaware of his presence, and took away the necklace, which protected her virginity. Then he put his arms around her naked body and lifted her from the fountain. Forgetting the stag and his dogs he betrothed her on the spot, and that same night the marriage was consummated under the open sky near the fountain. During the silence of the deep night, the nymph, whose virginity was gone, consulted the stars and learned that she would give birth to six sons and a daughter. She fearfully told this to her husband, who consoled her with his embraces and words. In the morning he returned to his castle with his wife.

When the mother of the young man saw the nymph and learned of their marriage, she believed that her influence and honor would be lessened, and her mind was twisted with hatred. She tried in many ways to sow seeds of hatred between them and destroy her son's love. But she could accomplish nothing, since her son paid no attention to her words and even became very angry with her. She then turned to other methods and conceived an impious crime, awful to relate, which she concealed within the dark chambers of her heart until the proper moment arose. In order to accomplish this crime better she concealed this deadly enmity and hatred within her soul and outwardly exhibited a kind face to her daughter-in-law. She honored her as the mistress of the castle and loved and cherished her as a daughter.

The nymph's pregnancy advanced until it was her time to give birth. As she had predicted previously she bore six sons and a daughter, each child having a golden necklace around its neck. These she happily (or rather I should say unhappily) entrusted to the wicked mother-in-law. Then the wicked woman seized the opportunity and accomplished what she had previously planned. She stole the seven children, and near the bed of the sleeping nymph she put seven puppies born nine days before. She gave the babies to a certain faithful servant and made him swear that he would strangle and bury them or drown them. He promised that he would do exactly as she wished, took them into the woods, and placed them under a tree. When he was preparing to strangle them he was restrained from the crime by pity or horror and instead left them under the tree, thinking to himself that he had carried out the order faithfully enough and kept his hands guiltless.

But God, the founder and begetter of all things, who sees all, and sustains and governs all, especially the race of men, did not forget that those little children were His handiwork. He sent them a guardian as soon as the servant had left, a certain old man who had chosen to live in the woods instead of the city to study philosophy and who was living in a cave. He found them, picked them up as if they were his own, and took them to the cave, bringing them up for seven years on the milk of a hind.

In the meantime, while the children were being carried into the woods by the aforesaid slave, the wicked old woman called her son and said, "Come, my son, and see what beautiful and noble children your wife has given birth to." She showed him the puppies, complaining that he had paid no attention to her words when she had warned him about the nymph. He believed his mother and was horrified at his wife. The burning love which he had formerly felt was turned to hatred. He ordered the puppies drowned, gave his wife no opportunity of explanation or denial, and ordered her to be buried alive up to the breasts in the courtyard of the palace. He ordered all the knights, the servants, the buffoons and hangers-on to wash their hands over the head of his wife and dry them on her hair before they took their meals. She was to be fed nothing except food thrown to the dogs.

She remained in this condition for seven years. Her clothing rotted away and her beautiful limbs were exposed, her snow white complexion turned black, her face became leathery, her eyes sank, her forehead wrinkled, her hair was foul and her flesh was eaten away. Only the skin was left stretched over her bones.

During those seven years that old philosopher had brought her children up well on hind's milk and the meat of birds and animals which they caught hunting. At this time by the dispensation of Providence their father chanced to go to the woods to hunt and there unexpectedly saw the children, who were wearing the golden necklaces. Moved by a natural emotion, he began to follow them as they fled, wishing to catch them. But they suddenly vanished before his eyes. He returned frustrated to the castle and told his mother and the others what he had seen. Her guilty conscience was aroused and she summoned the servant and asked if he had killed the children or left them alive. He admitted that he had left them alive but had placed them under a tree where they would soon die. "Indeed," she said, "my son saw them today. Unless you find them quickly and somehow take away their necklaces, you and I are lost."

The servant was as concerned for himself as for his mistress and hastened to the woods to seek the children. For three days he searched through the deep forest, and at last on the fourth day he found them transformed into swans. They were playing in a river, and their sister was guarding their necklaces on the bank. While they were swimming here and there as they played, the sister's attention was on them, and the servant, moving furtively, came upon her unawares and stole the necklaces. He was unable, however, to steal hers. Then he joyfully returned to his mistress and gave her the necklaces.

She summoned a goldsmith and ordered him to make a goblet from them. When the goldsmith had taken the necklaces he tried to melt them with fire, but it was impossible. Then he tried to break them with a hammer, but he was wasting his time. Neither fire nor iron affected them, with the exception of a ring of one of the necklaces which was bent a little. When he realized that nothing would do, he weighed the necklaces and put them away in his house. Then he took some gold of his own and made a goblet of the same weight as the necklaces. He gave it to the old woman who immediately put it in a box. She never drank from it or showed it to her son or anyone else.

As I said, the boys were transformed into swans. They could not regain their human shape without the necklaces. They were changed into swans, and with their sweet voices as fate decreed they bewailed their lot for a long time with their sister, who had been changed into a cygnet. They flew up,[44] and rising into the sky with their powerful wings they went to look for a lake or stream where they could live. When they had flown through the empty air a long time, they saw a lake of amazing length and width next to a certain castle. They were delighted by its beauty and settled upon it, happy to have found a suitable place. This was their father's castle which had been built on the natural cliff of a steep mountain, so that it was almost completely surrounded by the lake. The cliff, jutting out of the mountain, was so high that it seemed to stick to the clouds rather than the earth. On one side of the mountain there was only a very difficult and narrow ascent to it; on the other side it extended completely over the lake, so that if you could see the cliff hanging from above you would think that it and all the great buildings on it were about to fall into the depths. The palace was built on this part of it, with windows overlooking the lake.

The lord of the castle, deep in thought,[45] had just approached those windows, when suddenly he saw the birds on the lake, a type he had never seen before. He was delighted by their beauty and sweetness of voice and ordered the household not to frighten them but to throw them food and the remains from the table every day. He thought that this would cause them to become accustomed to the lake and remain there. After this had been done by the servants for a few days the birds became so tame that every day at meal time they would come to the shore and eagerly await their usual food. It was pleasant and delightful to watch them chase the half-eaten bread or bits of fish[46] in the waters of the lake.

The little girl, the sister of the swans, now in human form, had climbed to the castle and as an orphan was begging her daily food. She kept whatever crumbs she received from her father's table and shared them with the nymph who, as I said, was buried up to the breasts in the courtyard of the palace. By a natural affection she wept for her, not knowing it was her own mother. If there was any food left she took it to her brothers on the shore of the lake. When the swans saw her coming they would fly to her and, beating their wings and singing, would joyfully take the food brought by their sister, who kissed and embraced them. Every night she would return to the castle to sleep beside her mother, although as I said she did not know her. Everyone saw her go daily to the lake and divide what she had begged with the swans. They also saw her weeping over the buried nymph and wondered, saying that she seemed to resemble the nymph before she had lost her beauty.

When the lord of the castle saw the girl he was compelled by natural affection to look at her frequently. Finally he summoned her, looking at her carefully and noticing a certain resemblance to his own family. The golden necklace around her neck also attracted his attention. Then, thinking of the nymph, he said, "Tell me, little girl, who you are and where you come from. Who are your parents, and how are you able to summon the swans to you from the lake?"

Sighing and weeping she replied, "My lord, if nature permitted anyone to be born or exist without having parents, I would say that I do not know whether I had a mother or a father. I have never seen them, nor do I know anyone who has seen or known them. The swans about whom you ask me are my brothers. We were all born at the same time." Then she told him how they had been found by the old philosopher and brought up for seven years on hind's milk, how her brothers had lost their necklaces when bathing in the river and could not return to human shape, and how they had decided to settle on that lake.

That old woman—the sink of all iniquity, the worst of the worst—was there. The wicked servant, who had carried out her orders, was there, too. At the words of the girl they glanced at each other, and their guilt was obvious. Their confusion betrayed the secret crime. At some time good and evil are always exposed. God, the begetter and parent of all things, sees all things. Nothing escapes His knowledge. He does not suffer the innocent to perish or the unjust to glory in their wickedness.[47] He permitted the bloody minds of the old woman and the servant to be aroused to such a peak that they tried to kill the little girl. While she was going to the lake in her usual fashion, the servant followed. Drawing his sword he attacked her. As she fled, the lord of the castle, by chance returning from the field, came upon the servant from the rear and knocked the naked sword from his hand. Terrified of death, he quickly disclosed the secret crime and told what had happened, crying that he had only followed his mistress' orders.

Why say more? In addition he summoned his wicked mother and twisted out the truth by torture. The golden goblet, which was supposed to have been made from the necklaces, was taken out of the box. The goldsmith was summoned and asked whether he had made the goblet from the necklaces. He admitted what he had done and returned the necklaces. The happy girl took them to her brothers at the lake and gave each one his own. All were restored to human shape except the one whose ring the goldsmith had broken. He could not be restored but remained with one of his brothers as a swan. This is the swan about whom the story was told long ago that he drew with his golden necklace an armed soldier in a boat.[48] The father recognized and welcomed his children, and they their father. The nymph was taken from her grave and her beauty restored with baths and ointments and various poultices. According to the judgement of a wise man the foul old woman who had conceived and perpetrated such iniquity was forced to undergo the punishment to which the nymph had been condemned. Thus she fell into the pit which she had dug.

"Consider, O King, how great is the evil of woman. Take my advice and grant my request. Spare your innocent son. Realize that the naked truth may then more quickly appear."

The wise man had not yet finished his request when the queen, raging like a lioness who has lost her cubs, burst into view. "Throw me! me! into the flames!" she shouted, "O most unjust of all kings! Throw me in because I would not endure your son's lust and because I was not silent. Spare your criminal son! Have you influenced these crazy old men to make up these dreams so that you can save your wanton son and destroy me, the innocent one?"

When King Dolopathos heard these insults he could bear it no longer. He lifted his hands to the skies and swore by the gods that he himself would throw his son into the flames. Then the words and the cries of all the people rose on high. The whole plain echoed and re-echoed with shouts and weeping. Already the father had lifted his son from the earth with his own hands, already he was trying to throw him into the flames when suddenly Virgil, riding on a giant bird, came like lightning through the midst of the people and interrupted his attempt, shouting: "Stop! O King, take your hands off an innocent man! The laws forbid killing an innocent man! Renew the trial. He has been falsely accused and unjustly condemned contrary to the laws."

At this Lucinius, who had now seen and heard his teacher, awoke as if from a dream. At last he broke his deep silence. "Greetings, my teacher," he said. When the father heard his son speak he was astounded. All the kings and nobles wondered and stood amazed. On all sides the people ran up to listen and like stupid asses with uplifted ears stayed there.

Virgil began a bitter denunciation of the queen. "O madness," he cried, "O wickedness, O baseness, O evil woman, O woman truly a monster more monstrous than all monsters! Who has ever seen or heard such wickedness! Who has ever known or thought anything like this? I have read that Deianira poisoned Hercules! I have read that Clitemnestra slaughtered Agamemnon! But those crimes are less than hers. I could scarcely believe what I heard: that a woman had beaten the devil at his own game; that no evil was worse than hers! What wise man could outwit her? Who could understand the abyss of her heart? Who could guard her, unless she wished it? A bronze tower could not hold her, iron chains could not restrain her; bars and gates could not prevail over her plans. Through her kings totter, wars arise, cities fall, lands are devastated, and much noble blood is shed. Anger, quarrels, hatred, slander, jealousy, conflicts and rivalry come from woman! But why go on? The whole world was lost through a woman. A woman is a great evil.

The Story of Virgil

The Well

"But wait, something I saw has just occurred to me, how a certain philosopher was deceived by a woman. When he wished to marry and asked my advice about this I tried to dissuade him in every way, saying it was not fitting for a philosopher to take a wife. A woman is a great hindrance to philosophy. No one can control her actions. I also mentioned other objections which Theophrastus put in his Little Golden Book.[49]

"He replied that he had thought of a plan to avoid all her treachery. So he married against my advice and built a stone tower with only one small door and one small window. Here he shut his wife and permitted no man or woman to approach her. He always carried the key of the door with him, and whether he stayed within or went outside he always locked the door. When he slept he put the key under his head. In this way he guarded her jealously and diligently for a few days.

"One day when she was alone in the tower, she looked out the window and saw a young man sitting before the door of the house across the street. The more she watched him the more she fell in love with him. She did not try to restrain her blazing lust but beckoned to him. She threw down a note to him from the window which said that she wished to speak to him, mentioned her passion, and named the place and the exact time. She warned him to let no one know. He nodded his head in agreement and joyfully departed.

"She knew what she was doing. When the philosopher returned later he found her face more beautiful than usual, her embraces tighter and her kisses more alluring. She flattered him with sweet words, and finally while he dallied in useless pleasures of this kind she made him drunk with strong drink. But why go on? He became drunk and fell into a deep sleep. She stole the key, unbarred the door, ran to her young man, and wallowed for a long time in the pleasure she desired. While she was with her lover, her husband slept off the effect of the drink and awoke. He sadly realized that his wife had deceived him. Immediately he went to the door and locked it on the inside with very strong bolts so that it would not open when she was finished with adultery.

"On her return she found the door bolted and her husband awake. With tearful words she begged her husband to open the door, promising never to sin again. He refused and swore that tomorrow he would drag her publicly before her friends and the judges to be punished as an adultress. Shouting that she was going to drown herself in a nearby well she threw a big stone into it and then hid in the shadow of a statue.

"The philosopher heard the sound and thought she really had drowned herself. He quickly opened the door, ran to the well, put a pole down it, and tried to get his wife out. While he was uselessly doing this at the well, she suddenly jumped into the house and closed and barred the door, accusing her husband of what she had done. The tables were turned and the trapped philosopher had to beg her to open the door. He promised that he would never again lock her up and guard her against her will. Finally she reluctantly permitted him to enter. He tore down the tower and gave his wife the opportunity to go where she wished.

"And now I see a greater evil in this woman here, who, pretending to feel pity for the king, undertook to cure his son. But because he would not yield to her lust she claimed that he attacked her. Now to put an end to this affair, I say that you, O King, and you, O nobles, sentenced Lucinius contrary to the laws. He was mute and could not explain or defend himself when he was condemned. Although the laws state the punishment for each crime, in no case do they take away a man's right to defend himself or explain. They can condemn no deaf or mute person unless his guilt is obvious to all, because a dumb man is not able to defend himself or explain, and a deaf man cannot hear his accuser."

Then Lucinius was freed by the order of Virgil. His clothes were returned to him, at Virgil's urging he told what had happened: how he had left his teacher, and the order he had received; how the queen and her attendants had tried to incite him to lust; and how they had plotted against him by rending their faces, hair, and clothing with their nails. At this all the people cried out against the queen and her attendants, and in that very place without delay their own parents and relatives threw them into the flames, and they were burned alive. Thus they fell into the pit which they had dug, and into the noose which they had stretched, and received a punishment worthy of their crimes. Amid the rejoicing of all, Lucinius returned to the palace, and the king's crown was placed upon his head. He received the homage and fealty of the kings and nobles, and then all were permitted to return home.

King Dolopathos died that year, as did Virgil. As the latter was dying he clutched in his hands the two handbooks which he had written about the arts. After his death no one could make him relax his grip. Some said he did this because of jealousy. Others say he did it so that everyone could not easily learn the liberal arts and thus cheapen them, else the proper reverence would not be paid to those who mastered them. Lucinius burned their bodies in the pagan manner and put their bones in golden urns. He placed his father's bones in Palermo and his teacher's in the city of Mantua.

But before I pass on to other things, it is proper to consider a little the virtues of the father and the son. Consider how great was the justice of the father when he applied the laws to his only son. What strength ruled him, who could suffer his only son to perish! And what shall I say of the son? Should I praise the manner in which he obeyed the order of his teacher, or should I admire his firmness, his endurance, and his chastity? Amid the praise of the actors and the embellishment of the mimes he did not forget the command of his teacher. Amid the speeches of kings and nobles, amid the greetings of noble women, he did not break the silence imposed upon him. Amid so many witches (I mean the queen and her attendants) he kept the command and his chastity. Seven times he was accused, seven times condemned, yet he kept the command. When he was brought to the flames, he showed great firmness. He did not change expression, he did not look away, he did not weep, he did not tremble, he was not afraid, but always stood firm and calm. Today what kings and nobles, or even abbotts, could equal the justice of the father? What poor monks, not to speak of worldly men, could equal the obedience and endurance of the son? But so much for this. I would not seem to attempt to extol with my praises those whom their own deeds have made famous.

After Lucinius had gained complete control of the kingdom and his father's affairs, he governed well and peacefully even to the final days of the rule of Tiberius Caesar, showing himself a king as well as a philosopher in bearing, features, and morals. Now at that time the truth had already been born in the world. The Word[50] had already sprung from the bosom of the Father. Our Lord Jesus Christ had already suffered, risen from the dead, and ascended into Heaven. Already His apostles and disciples were preaching the evangel through all the world. One of the Roman Jews who believed in Christ had come to Sicily to preach, and by chance was staying in the same city as Lucinius. He was preaching Christ zealously, saying that He was the Creator and savior of all men, very god of very god, created before the world from the word of the Father; that He had recently been born of a virgin, suffered, was crucified and died for the redemption of mankind; that He arose on the third day and ascended into Heaven, from where He would return to judge each one according to his works and give glory to the good, eternal punishment to the evil.[51] He said that the idols they worshipped were useless. They were deaf and dumb and dead. They could give no aid to their worshippers, and they were not gods but rather the abode of demons.

The citizens were stunned at this new and unusual preaching and hastened to the king, to tell him that a certain man of despicable appearance was preaching some new religion in the forum. The king summoned him and asked him from what nation he came, his race, whether he was slave or free, and what he professed. The holy man, answering each of the questions, said that he was a Roman, a Jew by race, a free man, and a Christian.

King Lucinius, continuing, said, "What is this new superstition you are trying to introduce? Who is this new god of yours, whose name is still unknown to us, whom you urge us to worship to the neglect of our own great ones? Do you not know that it is against the Roman law to dare to introduce a new god without the consent of the senate and the nobles?"

"O illustrious and wise king," said the holy man, "I do not preach a new god but an ancient one, whom your philosophers call the highest good and the begetter of all things. He created the sky, the land, the sea, and all things contained in them, not from pre-existing or co-eternal matter, but from nothing. Very recently it was His will to become flesh and be born of a virgin for the redemption of lost humanity.[52] But since I know you are a philosopher and see you interested in what I say, may we depart to some private place for a little while? When I disclose to you, who are very discriminating, the mysteries of our redemption and salvation, I would not wish those mysteries to cause disbelief rather than wonder in those of weak intellect."

Wishing to hear the words of the holy man, King Lucinius took him into a private chamber and when all others were absent he said, "Now we have no witness. Tell me what you promised: how man was lost and how it was necessary that the creator of all things become the thing created for our salvation."

"O illustrious one," answered the holy man, "please let me begin our discussion a little earlier in time. Then you can more easily understand how gloriously man was created, how he fell and was condemned in this world, and how he has been saved. Well then, God, the beginning of all things, who is Himself without a beginning, created the heavens, the earth, and the sea, not from any shapeless or pre-existing matter, which Plato called *hyle*, but from nothing, as I said before.[53] From these He made the beauty of the sun and the moon and the stars,[54] the beauty of the four-footed beasts and birds and fish,[55] the beauty of the trees and plants.[56] When He had made the world and arranged it properly, the great Maker was pleased with His work, and all things seemed good to His eyes. But since there was no one to take delight in this beauty, the supremely good One, who was without jealousy, wished to have someone with whom He could share the wealth of His glory and goodness. So in His deep wisdom he formed a certain superior animal in His own image and likeness, excelling the others—man. Into it He breathed a divine spirit, which the other animals lacked, a reasoning soul with which he would know how to preserve the grace of his Father and distinguish good from evil. He also made a helper for him—woman, similar to him throughout.[57] Nor did He wish to create them with four feet, or mute, or having eyes looking downward, but erect, capable of speech, and holding their eyes upward. For

Other animals look down upon the earth
But He gave to man a lofty face and ordered him
To lift his features upward to the sky[58]

so that he might have his eyes fixed upon Him who had honored him
with origin and first rank. Of all the things which He had created
under the sky, man was the most beautiful and the most wise. He
made him the master and put him and his wife in a garden of delight
planted eastward in Eden with all kinds of trees and plants. It contained also the tree of life, and he who tasted of this would never die.
There was also the tree of knowledge of good and evil.[59] As I said,
He placed man in the garden to enjoy it without labor and to live in
it without pain until taken to a better place. In addition, He permitted them to eat of the fruit of all the trees of paradise, with the exception of the tree of knowledge of good and evil. This He forbade,
saying that if they ever dared to taste of it they would surely die.[60]

"But they did not long obey the command of their Creator. They
had scarcely been there seven hours when the devil, who had been
damned on account of the pride with which he was swollen against
God, grew envious of the glory and happiness of the man. Using the
mouth of a snake he urged the woman, since she was the weaker, to
eat of the fruit of the forbidden tree, lying that when they had eaten
the fruit they would become immortal and be like gods, knowing
good and evil. He said that God denied them the fruit of this tree
from envy. The woman was deceived and tricked. She ate of the tree
and gave to the man who did eat also.[61] Immediately both realized of
what good they had been deprived, and into what evil they had
fallen. But why go on? Judgment was passed immediately upon our
first parents. They were expelled from that garden of delight and cast
down into this vale of misery and shadow.[62] Paradise was enclosed
with a wall and a fiery expanse of waters."

"Did God know in advance that man would sin?" asked Lucinius.

"Certainly," said the holy man. "He knew, and He knew before He
created the world. He foresaw what each thing would be like. The
eye of His majesty also sees and understands the past and the future
as if they were the present."

"But," said Lucinius, "if He knew in advance that man would fall, why did He create one who could fall? Why did He plant that tree which allowed man to sin and caused his damnation, especially if He is supremely good, as you and Plato call him? If He knew in advance and could have prevented the fall, but did not do so, He must be guilty of man's damnation. In that case He is not supremely good. On the other hand, if He wished to do so and could not, then we may justly accuse Him of weakness. But if He permitted or wished man to fall so that He could lift him up again, then He seems to me futile or stupid. A carpenter is justly accused of stupidity if he deliberately builds a house badly so that he can rebuild it after it has fallen."

The man of God replied, "God so made man that he could remain immortal if he wished. He gave him an order and promised two rewards for obedience or disobedience, immortality or death. Life if he kept the order, death if he did not. Between these two He put a mean, so to speak, giving him free will so that he could freely choose, without coercion, one of the two. God's grace helped him to choose the better and reject the worse. Man, however, used his free will wrongly. Compelled by nothing or no one, he voluntarily surrendered his weapons, that is the grace of God, and yielded to the enticing words of the tempter. If he had resisted temptation even a little, at this evidence of obedience he would have been transferred immediately to a better state and strengthened in the good, for God seeks just opportunities to glorify men. Even as the good angels were strengthened when the evil angels fell, so man would have become immortal. But because he willingly and without compulsion ignored the order of God, he was condemned by the just judgment of God. The tree of knowledge of good and evil was planted not to destroy man but to glorify him, so that his restraint would make him worthy of greater glory. God knew in advance the fall of man, but He neither preordained nor wished it. He forbade him to sin under the threat of death because, since He is supremely good, He wishes no evil, only the good. Since God is supremely good, He is also omnipotent and supremely just. The just can do or wish nothing except what is completely just. Although God is supremely good and supremely powerful, yet He can do or wish nothing except what His own highest justice enjoins. It was not just to save man, who voluntarily sinned of his own free will. Therefore God could not and did not wish to save man because it was not just to save one who could easily protect himself with the help of God's grace. In this way He can and cannot be called omnipotent. He can wish and not wish, since He is able to do everything which is just and is not able to do whatever is unjust. He wishes everything good and nothing evil. Because of this He wishes every evil to be a sin and a sin to be nothing. Since God, without whom nothing exists, cannot do or wish evil, we have proved that a sinner is condemned by God, not without reason, but because his will and purpose are contrary to God's. Nor must you think that He stupidly, futilely, and deliberately created man weak so that He could restore him after the Fall. He arranges and governs all things with strength and wisdom. He has created everything beautiful, perfect, and good; and man He has made better than all in virtue, wisdom, and beauty. But disregarding his worthiness and casting aside his weapons, so to speak, he fell of his own free will and knowledge, by his own fault. God, therefore, justly allowed him to fall, because he had cast himself down and He has been supremely merciful to offer salvation to the justly condemned.

"Can a vessel made of clay say to the potter, 'Why did you make me this way?' No. He makes one vessel beautiful, another ugly, as he wishes. So God, the moulder of men,[63] mercifully shares His kingdom and honor with one, but He spurns another and delivers him as food for the eternal fires. Although God's judgment is secret, it is just."

"I agree with what you say," said Lucinius, "but let me know more clearly how man was justly condemned."

He replied, "If a traveler was walking on a wide road in the middle of which there was a deep well, if he had been warned about the danger, yet of his own will walked in the middle of the road and fell into it, tell me who would mourn him? Who could justly give him a hand? Who would mourn stupid Empedocles, who wished to be thought a god and so voluntarily leaped into blazing Aetna?[64] So it is with man who sinned of his own free will, without force."

"These things have been reasonably presented," said Lucinius, "but now tell me how man has been redeemed."

The holy man replied: "When our first parents, as I said, broke the command of God they were thrust from the blessedness in which they had been created and fell into this vale of misery—mortal and fragile life. Cursed by God, they exchanged the delights of paradise to live in this condemned earth. Their children, wandering like wild beasts, were scattered throughout the world. They did not have cities and companionship, morals and integrity, laws and a just life. They had never even heard the names of the arts and philosophy and prophecy but wandered through the wilderness and the solitudes with no fixed homes. If the mercy of their Maker had planted any seeds of goodness in them, they left these seeds untilled and untouched and followed the road of evil on its downward path.[65] So it happened that they committed foul crimes against each other. Sometimes they were attacked, sometimes they were murdered. Their savagery even went to the extent of eating each other. Those stories which tell of the battles of the gods and the giants are the records of their crimes. Finally their foul deeds aroused the divine vengeance, which overwhelmed them with a flood[66] and destroyed them with rains of fire and checked the savagery and impiety of this world with many other penalties.

"Yet it seemed best to the Creator to correct rather than destroy the human race, although it was corrupted by the infectious disease of evil. He pitied their souls, which were dark with evil and hindered by blindness. At times the Creator used the intervention of His angels and servants, at times miracles. Sometimes God even deemed it worthwile to appear Himself. If anywhere He found a few men still mindful of Him and justice, He instructed them properly by divine revelations and sound advice and teaching. Through those men He tried to reshape the human race and recall it from darkness, since only by means of a man could men be taught and corrected and helped.

"Gradually a pure race known as the Hebrews began to revere and worship Him. They were at first uncivilized and infected by their former life, but through Moses the prophet He established the elements, so to speak, of a more holy learning which was to come. This law,[67] like the beginning of light, gleamed over the world and filled all the lands and seas with its fragrant odor. In different parts of the world wise men, legislators, and philosophers gradually began to teach to their followers its orderly and basic precepts, filled with honor and justice. They summoned the wild and fierce customs of men to propriety and honesty. The laws of Cecrops[68] and other laws took their beginning from this. Men were taught to form friendships and to make treaties of peace. Then men learned to help each other and to share, and when they were suitably trained and ready for the divine precepts, they became able to grasp the knowledge of God, the Father of all things.

"Finally the time came when the Creator of man decided to redeem mankind. The One who is the teacher of all virtue, who is the communication and the doctrine, the word and the wisdom of God, who in the beginning with His Father created man, He, I say, assumed the substance of human nature and the lowly form of man. He differed from us only in that He was without sin. He had permitted the power of the Roman Empire under Augustus Caesar to extend far and wide. Born of a virgin, He entered the world just as we do, but without a human father. As the inspired prophets had divinely preached, He taught men the holiness of His Father and showed by numerous miracles that He was both God and man. Finally, to redeem mankind He was crucified by the treacherous Jews. On the third day He rose and remained forty days with His disciples. Eating and drinking with them He proved the true resurrection of the flesh. At last He sent His disciples forth to baptize and preach to the Gentiles and then as they watched He ascended into Heaven on clouds of glory, whence we await his return to judge us."[69]

"I would like to know," said Lucinius, "why He did not become known to all people before this and why faith and knowledge of Him did not come to all."

"The world was still too crude and ignorant to understand the perfect doctrine of Christ," replied the holy man. "Men differed little, if at all, from the brute beasts. As proof of this, there are some who say that men were first made by Prometheus,[70] a wise man, who was able to change their fierce ways and great ignorance into kindness and knowledge. As Horace says:

Orpheus, the holy mouthpiece of the gods is said to have recalled savage man from murder and a brutal life, and to have tamed wild tigers and lions.

Amphion, the founder of Thebes, is said to have moved stones with the sound of his lyre, and with sweet music to lead them where he willed.[71]

The same poet says that:

In the beginning when the mute and shapeless animals crawled forth, men fought them with their nails, and fists, and clubs for food and shelter. Finally they used weapons which they made. Then their voices found and formed the words for things, and this caused them to cease their battles, to build cities and pass laws against theft, and banditry, and adultery.[72]

"When some of your own prophets considered the arrangement of the sky and the earth, the harmony and disharmony of the elements, the change of seasons, and the movement of the planets, they realized that there was a god who governed these things. When they had learned this, however, they did not glorify Him as God but became lost in their own thoughts. Their hearts became foolish, and they served the creature rather than the Creator.[73] They fell among false angels and worshiped them as gods. Adherents of various errors rose up and each one swore he knew the truth. But their ideas about the creation of the world and its creator were so different and diverse that they were justly condemned. Aristotle proposes four principles in the creation of the world: coeternal beginnings, matter and maker, form, which he calls *eidos*, and the plan of the maker. Plato proposes five: matter, maker, shape, plan of the maker, and idea, or exemplar. Thales of Miletus proposes two: fire and water. Epicurus also proposes two: void and atoms. He also asserts that the four elements are made from the atoms and that the world revolves by chance without a maker. If his opinion were true, this world, which consists of contrary parts, would long ago have returned to its old chaos. Some of the Stoics add two principles: matter and maker. Others propose three: time when, place where, and movement by which God created the world. Now how could they speak the truth when they believed so many different things? Truth cannot consist of diversity."[74]

"What necessity was there that God should suffer so cruel a form of death for man when He could have freed him by a man or by an angel?" asked Lucinius.

"God was not forced," he replied. "But it was His pity, His intent, and His will that he who had first conquered man be in turn conquered by one who was both man and God. Neither angel nor mortal man was suitable for this."

Lucinius said, "It certainly seems to me unworthy and foolish for God to endure these things on behalf of man."

"Do not call this foolish," he replied, "but consider the worthiness of God. Consider how much He loved man, whom He wished to redeem at no other price than His own blood. On behalf of man He voluntarily became a man, but He did not lose His divine nature; rather He imparted His divine nature to us. He became what He was not, but He remained what He was. Because of this, one of us Christians has cleverly said this about Him and His mother the Virgin:

> I am what I was, I was not what I am, I have become both.[75]

"Since our first parents had broken the first command, He imposed another: baptism, which is brought about by water and the Holy Spirit and made effective through confession and the invocation of the Holy Trinity. By the confession of the Holy Trinity He also excused the triple sin of Eden: pride, which despised the command of God; gluttony, which desired the forbidden fruit; greed, which wished to be God."

"What do you mean by the Holy Trinity?" asked Lucinius.

"One God in three Persons," he answered. "I do not preach three principles to you but one single God by whom all things were created, not from previous matter, as Plato says, but from nothing. We distinguish the trinity by three names: Father, Son, and Holy Ghost, that is, power, wisdom, and gracious purpose. These three things, the ability, the knowledge, and the will must be in harmony if any Creator decides to make something. But if one of them is lacking, nothing can be accomplished. When these three things exist in a man, you do not say there are three men instead of one. Thus we profess one God worshipped in three attributes: to the Father (the source) we assign omnipotence, to the Son (through whom all things are) we assign wisdom, to the Holy Spirit (in whom all things are) we assign graciousness. Although in addition the Father is wise, and the Son is powerful, and the Holy Spirit is wise, the Son is equal to the Father, and the Holy Spirit is co-eternal and co-equal to the Father and the Son. But I dare not discourse further about this ineffable and individual trinity, especially since you are a pagan and perhaps incredulous. This is as far above us as the Creator is above the thing created. I could not find the proper words to say what I know and feel in my heart. Indeed, I would be overwhelmed by the glory. My mind fails me when I consider its majesty."

"Your words please me," said Lucinius, "but now I would like to know if the false angels, whom you said fell, will ever find mercy as man has found it."

"They never will find mercy," said the holy man, "because they do not seek it. Their nature is always engaged in evil, hardened by the just judgment of God. Unlike man, they were created of the finest substance and were not weighed down with earthly matter. They sinned against their Creator because of their own evil nature. No one urged or impelled them, and so they are justly condemned for eternity. But man, who was weighed down with his own flesh, sinned because of an evil angel. He has obtained pardon from a merciful God."

"You have given me a reasonable answer," Lucinius said. "Now I would like to know what you think about our gods."

At this he said, "What else than what the poet Virgil thinks:

fear first created gods in the world.[76]

Those statues made of gold, silver, wood, stone, and metal began in the time of Ninus, who was the first man to wage war against other people. He set up a tyranny and tried to remain master by murder. When he could not bear the grief occasioned by the death of his father Belus,[77] he made a beautiful statue of him and tried to temper (or rather feed) his grief a little with this. Every day it was his custom to worship the statue on bended knees, but while he was merely trying to relieve his grief he offered a mistaken and deadly example. Other powerful men throughout the world imitated him and set up statues to their parents and their dear ones. Criminals, who feared that their masters would execute them for their crimes, began to flee to the statues, for whose sake they were pardoned. They began to consider those images, which had saved them from death, as gods, and gradually this error increased on the earth.

"Demons, which always envy the safety of men and work for their destruction, increased this error by assuming human form. They taught black magic and idolatry and even inhabited the statues and pretended they were gods. Sometimes they deluded men with false prophecies, as once the Delphic Apollo deceived Pirrus the king of Epirus with the ambiguous line: 'I say, O son of Aeacus, that you the Romans can conquer.'[78] This can be taken in two ways: he could conquer the Romans, or be conquered by them. If war was declared, one or the other would certainly happen.

"Finally, tyrants and men who committed outstanding crimes were called gods. There is Saturn, who ate his own children. And Jove, who drove his father from the throne and changed himself into a bull, or a swan, or a shower of gold to commit adultery with women. Mars is a thief, Bacchus gets dead drunk and snores, and Venus fornicates with Mars, or Vulcan, or Anchises, and who knows how many? How can you call them gods, when you would be ashamed to imitate their life and actions? Wretched men have even worshipped the elements, the sun, the moon, the planets. All these things move or stop at the will and decision of their maker. And men worship other things: animals, bulls, asses, goats, apes, trees, and even onions; especially the Egyptians, whose great stupidity is manifest.[79] Hear what our lyric poet and prophet, King David, said about your gods:

But our God is in the heavens. He hath done whatsoever He hath pleased. Their idols are silver and gold, the work of men's hands. They have mouths, but they speak not: eyes have they, but they see not: they have ears, but they hear not: noses have they, but they smell not: they have hands, but they handle not: feet have they, but they walk not: neither speak they through their throat.

They that make them are like unto them; so is everyone that trusteth in them.[80]

That is those without feeling. And another prophet, Isaiah, mocks the idols and their worshippers. He says:

The carpenter heweth down a tree; yea, he kindleth it and baketh bread. And the residue thereof he maketh a god, even his graven image; he falleth down unto it, and worshippeth it, and prayeth unto it, and saith, Deliver me, for thou art my god. He has not known nor understood, and he saith: I have burned part of it in the fire; yea, also I have baked bread upon the coals thereof; I have roasted flesh, and eaten it; and shall I make the residue thereof an abomination? Shall I fall down to the stock of a tree?[81]

And another prophet also says:

The gods that have not made the heavens and the earth, even they shall perish from the earth.[82]

And your poet, Horace, is he not laughing at the gods when he brings one on the stage talking about himself?

Once I was a fig tree's trunk, a useless log. The carpenter was in doubt whether to make me a stool or Priapus. He decided on the latter. So I became a god. I frighten thieves and birds. My right hand and this big, red pole sticking out of my filthy groin keep away thieves."[83]

Lucinius said, "You might persuade men to desert their gods completely and worship your Christ if you could show that some of the philosophers had knowledge of Him. But when you present only the evidence of some unknown men or other, I can't tell whether it is true or false."

"You could rightly accuse me of falsehood," he replied, "if I didn't produce evidence about our Lord Christ from your own sources. First I refer you to the words of the Tiburtine Sibyl. When Augustus desired to know whether he should accept the decree of the senate which named him god and lord, the reply bore witness to the truth of Christ. For after she had spent three days awake and fasting in her secret place, she went to him and said, 'O Caesar, it will certainly happen that

the earth will drip moisture as a sign of judgment. A king incarnate will come from heaven who will endure forever and judge the world. Then believers and unbelievers will see god.'[84]

And there were other things she said which obviously refer to the
birth of Christ, His suffering and resurrection, and the future
judgment.

"In another place it says, 'God the Son gave God to the sons of men
to be worshipped. Know that your lord is the son of God.'⁸⁵ Christ
said from the cross, 'Thrice and four times blessed is the tree which
bears God.'⁸⁶ When your Virgil, who had an intimation of Chris-
tianity, writes: 'A new lineage now comes from the lofty sky,'⁸⁷ is he
not predicting Christ, who was to be born from a virgin a few years
later? And in the line before he even mentions a virgin: 'Now the
virgin and the days of Saturn return.' Consider the following words
of a father to his son: 'O my son, my strength, my power and
safety.'⁸⁸ And when Virgil wrote, 'Thinking such things he stopped
and was transfixed,'⁸⁹ he was predicting our Savior on the cross.

"Mercury, the son of Semele who is wrongly believed to mediate
between gods and men, wrote a book which has as its title *Logos
Telios*, that is, the Perfect Word. In this book he acknowledges that
he is a mortal, not a god, and that the true mediator between God
and men will be Jesus Christ, the Son of God. In this book he says:

The Lord God, Creator of all things, made a second lord. When he had
made this creation first and only and one and saw that it was good and filled
with his goodness, he rejoiced. He loved his only-begotten son whom he
first made and later called only-begotten. I am not the son of God. The son
of the blessed God and divine grace cannot be told in human speech.⁹⁰

"The great Socrates built an altar at Athens and inscribed on it: 'To
the Unknown God.'⁹¹ He worshipped only the god of the heavens
and wouldn't even give idols a name. When the fifty tyrants tried to
force him to worship Jove or Mercury, his strong soul would yield to
neither prayers, nor bribes, nor threats. He said that they were idols
made of silver, or gold, or wood, or stone. Because of his faith in
God they put him in prison and made him drink hemlock.

"In Egypt, too, the very ancient priests of Heliopolis placed in their
temple the image of a maiden holding a boy in her left arm. This was
a symbol to their descendants that when a virgin who had born a son

should enter the temple the idols of Egypt would fall. When Christ was born, Herod, the king of the province of Judea, wanted to kill the child, and his virgin mother fled with him into Egypt and entered the temple.[92] Immediately all the idols fell before her feet. The priests and men of the city carefully observed the virgin and the child and noticed that they resembled the image of the maiden and the boy. Then they honored the virgin and worshipped the boy as God.[93]

"At Rome when Christ was born the temple of Peace and Concord collapsed completely, on the lintel of which Romulus had written that it would not fall until a virgin had borne a son.[94] Whether he said this as a prophecy or merely meant that it was as impossible for the temple to fall as for a virgin to bear a son, you will consider. But it is established that when Christ was born of a virgin, the temple was overturned. Again at Rome across the Tiber when Christ was born a fountain of oil burst from the ground and flowed into the Tiber all day, symbolizing that the true oil, that is true mercy, had come from the earth, that is from a virgin.[95]

"On the day of Christ's crucifixion there was such a great earthquake that rocks were split, and an eclipse of the sun shadowed all the earth from the sixth to the ninth hour.[96] Phlego,[97] the famous calculator of the Olympiads, mentioned this: 'In the fourth year of the two hundred and second Olympiad, that is in the eighteenth year of the reign of Tiberius Caesar, there was an eclipse of the sun far greater than any before. From the sixth hour the day turned so dark that the stars were seen in the sky and an earthquake in Bithynia destroyed many cities of Nicea.' When all the Greek and Latin philosophers realized that the eclipse of the sun had happened at the improper time, that is on the fourteenth day of the lunar month in which the Jews celebrate Passover and during which they crucified Christ, they were confused because the usual time is on the thirtieth or first. Since they could discover no reason, they said that God, the Creator of nature, was suffering. Now are these proofs enough for you, O King, or do you wish more evidence supplied from your own people?"

"They are indeed enough," said Lucinius. "What you say is important and worthy of respect, but thick shadows cover my heart and do not permit me to see clearly the light of truth."

"I trust that the Lord will soon drive away these shadows by the light of His presence," said the holy man.

At these words there passed by the funeral of a certain noble youth whose body was being taken outside the city to be cremated in the manner of the pagans. A crowd of people, crying and weeping, was following the funeral. When Lucinius heard the weeping and realized the cause of their grief he said, "Reverend sir, you can drive out the cloud of disbelief from my heart if you can restore this youth in the name of your God."

Immediately the holy man, trusting in the power of Christ, ran and ordered them to put down the bier. He called upon the name of Christ and shouted, "Young man, by the power of Jesus Christ, our Savior, I say to you: Arise and preach to the people the power of God Almighty!"

And he who had been dead arose and praised Christ, saying that He was the only true God, and the idols were not gods but demons. Then a great group of people extolled and praised Jesus Christ, and the tears of the mourners were replaced with tears of joy.

On the same day Lucinius and a great number of people who believed in Christ were baptized, but he did not change his name. Since he wished to see the apostles of Christ he abdicated the rich throne of Sicily and appointed one of his most faithful friends in his place. He and the holy man walked to Jerusalem together. But what he did after that, whether he preached to the pagans with the other apostles or remained in the Holy Land, I do not know. I do know that he never returned to his kingdom. Some say that he remained near the holy places where Christ was born and suffered until the end of his life. Whatever he did, however, we trust in Him who called him to His faith and drew him to the places of His holy existence; that He guided his actions right to the end, and that He received him into the mansion of eternal rest.

This is the end of my story. I hope the reader will not think that I have written things incredible or impossible. Nor must he accuse me of imitating those whose faults I criticized in the preface of my book. These tales, which I did not read but heard, were written by me to please and instruct the reader. I hope I have accomplished my purpose. Even if they didn't really happen, they could have happened.

No one is forced to have my gift, I shall compel no one to read it.

But if, unjustly aroused with envy and jealousy, someone is displeased with my work and condemns it as false, let him tell me how the magi of Pharaoh changed their wands into snakes; how they brought the frogs from the swamps; how they turned the waters of the Nile to blood.[98] And let him tell me also how the Pythoness summoned the prophet Samuel;[99] how Circe, the daughter of the sun, changed the friends of Ulysses into different animals. The blessed Augustine and the Spaniard Isidore swear that these stories are true.[100] Since the reader cannot deny them, he must accept my story also.

Notes

Bibliography

Index Nominum

Notes to the Text

1. John 10: 12.
2. Matt. 8: 20.
3. Juv. *Sat.* 6. 165.
4. 2 Peter 1: 19.
5. Hor. *Epist.* 1. 18. 9; *Odes* 2. 10. 5.
6. Psalms 64: 14.
7. Joel 2: 24.
8. Num. 16: 13–14.
9. Verg. *G.* 3. 439; *Aen.* 2. 475.
10. Ovid *Rem. Am.* 81.
11. Ovid *Rem. Am.* 91–92.
12. Num. 22: 29–30.
13. Plato *Resp.* 473D; Lactant. *Div. Inst.* 3. 21.
14. Source unknown.
15. Hor. *Odes* 1. 3. 8; Ovid *Tr.* 1. 2. 44, 4. 10. 32.
16. Psalms 54: 16, 138: 7–10; Num. 16: 30.
17. He later is able to write a note to his father freeing Virgil and the ambassadors from guilt (p. 29). Why can't he write a note to his father later describing the perfidy of the queen? The same incongruity is found in the Latin version of the *Book of Sendebar*.
18. Juv. *Sat.* 6. 500–505.
19. Source unknown.
20. Ovid *Ex Ponto* 4. 3. 35–36.
21. Hor. *Odes* 4. 13–14.
22. Lucan *Pharsalia* 1. 70–71.
23. A reference to Phalaris, the tyrant of Agrigentum, who practiced this unhappy custom. Ovid *Ars Amatoria* 1. 653; Lactant. *Div. Inst.* 3. 27.
24. See footnote 17.
25. Job 31: 30.
26. Babrius *Fables* 143; Phaedrus *Fables* 20 (Loeb). *Die "Disciplina Clericalis" des Petrus Alfonsi, exemplum V*, ed. A. Hilka and W. Söderhjelm (Heidelberg, 1911).
27. Hor. *Odes* 1. 13. 5–8.
28. Verg. *Aen.* 4. 569–70.
29. Source unknown.
30. Lament. 1: 12.

31. Verg. *Aen.* 2. 1.
32. Hor. *Ars P.* 163–65.
33. Hor. *Ars P.* 162.
34. Hor. *Epist.* 1. 19. 8.
35. Source unknown.
36. The story of Rhampsinitos, first found in Herodotus *History* 2. 121.
37. Eccles. 10: 16. For another analogue to the story "The Old Man," cf. Hermann Oesterley, ed. *Gesta Romanorum* (Berlin: Weidmannsche Buchhandlung, 1872), Cap. 124, 473–75.
38. Matt. 10: 26; Psalms 51: 3; Jeremiah 13:23.
39. Verg. *Ecl.* 3. 93.
40. Ovid *Her.* 7. 6.
41. Verg. *Aen.* 5. 9.
42. Ovid *Ex Ponto* 4. 6. 47, *Met.* 15. 462; Hor. *Ars P.* 91, et alii.
43. Matt. 4: 2; Mark 1: 12; Luke 4: 2.
44. Alexander Neckam, *De naturis rerum*, xlix, p. 100 (ed. Wright).
45. Hor. *Sat.* 1. 9. 2.
46. Hor. *Sat.* 1. 3. 81.
47. Matt. 10: 26; Psalms 51: 3.
48. This may be a reference to Godfrey de Bouillon.
49. Theophrastus (ca. 370–285 B.C.), a pupil of Aristotle who carried on his work. Passages of the *Aureolus*, which is lost, can be found in Jerome *Against Jovinian*. Cf. also Walter Map *De nugis curialium* 4. 4.
50. John 1: 1.
51. Compare the Nicene Creed.
52. Matt. 1: 23; Luke 1: 27.
53. Gen. 1: 1–2.
54. Gen. 1: 14–18.
55. Gen. 1: 20–25.
56. Gen. 1: 11–12.
57. Gen. 1: 26–30.
58. Ovid *Met.* 1. 84–86.
59. Gen. 2: 8–9.
60. Gen. 2: 15–17.
61. Gen. 3: 1–6.
62. Gen. 3: 2–3.
63. Tertullian *Adversus Judaeos* 2.
64. Hor. *Ars P.* 464–66; Walter Map *De nugis curialium* 4. 3; Lactant. *Div. Inst.* 3. 18.
65. Gen. 6: 11–12.
66. Gen. 7: 10–24.
67. Exod. 20: 1–26.
68. A mythical first king of Athens.
69. Matt. 28: 17–20; Mark 16: 9–20; Luke 24: 15–53; John 20: 14–31, 21: 1–25.

70. A Titan who was supposed to have made mankind out of clay. He is also supposed to have given fire to man.

71. Hor. *Ars P.* 391–96.

72. Hor. *Sat.* 1. 3. 99–106.

73. Romans 1: 21.

74. Lactant. *Div. Inst.* 5. 3.

75. Source unknown.

76. This is not from Vergil but from Servius on Verg. *Aen.* 2. 715. It is also found in Statius *Theb.* 3. 661, and Petronius frag. 27.

77. Ninus and Belus, cf. Cyrillus Alex. *Adversus Julian* (Paris, 1638) 6. 110. In Greek mythology Ninus, the son of Belos (or Bel), was the eponymous founder of Nineveh.

78. Ennius *Annals* 6. 174–76 (Warmington); Quint. *Instit.* 7. 9. 6.

79. Pliny *HN* 19. 6.

80. Psalms 113: 3–8 (Vulgate); 115: 3–8 (King James).

81. Isaiah 44: 13–19.

82. Jeremiah 10: 11.

83. Hor. *Sat.* 1. 8. 1–5.

84. *Mirabilia Romae*, ed. Parthey (Berlin, 1869), p. 33; Rzack, *Oracula Sibyllina* (Vienna, 1891), p. 153.

85. Rzack, *Oracula Sibyllina*, p. 88.

86. Rzack, *Oracula Sibyllina*, p. 132.

87. Verg. *Ecl.* 4. 7.

88. Verg. *Aen.* 1. 664.

89. Verg. *Aen.* 2. 650.

90. Lactant. *Div. Inst.* 4. 6 and 7. 18; Hermes, p. 51a (Patricius); Pseudo-Apuleius, *Asclepius* 100. 26; Sedalius, p. 47; The Pseudo-Augustine, *Against Five Heresies*, in vol. 8, Appendix of the Maurist Edition of Augustine's works. Rzack, *Oracula Sibyllina*, p. 158.

91. Acts 17: 23. In this paragraph John must be indulging his sense of humor.

92. Matt. 2: 13–14.

93. Thilo, *Codex Apocryphus Novi Testamenti* (Leipzig, 1832) 1. 398 ("Historia de nativitate Mariae et de infantia Salvatoris," Cap. 22–23). E. Hennecke and W. Schneemelcher (translation ed. by R. McL. Wilson), *New Testament Apocrypha* (Philadelphia, 1963) 1: 66, 413; Isaiah 19: 1.

94. *Mirabilia Romae*, p. 55.

95. Eusebii Pamphili *Chronica*, ed. Scaliger (Leiden, 1601), p. 153; Petrus Comestor, *Hist. scholastica*, Ev. cap. 5.

96. Matt. 27: 51–52; Mark 15: 33; Luke 23: 44–45.

97. Jerome in Phlegonte. *Speculum humanae salvationis* 8.

98. Exod. 7: 9–22.

99. 1 Reg. 28: 7–25.

100. Augustine, *De civitate Dei* 18. 17–18. Isidore, *Etymologiarum* 8. 9.

Bibliography

A full bibliography can be found in the Newsletter of the Society of the Seven Sages, published by Hans R. Runte at Dalhousie University.

Artola, George. "The Nature of the *Book of Sindbād*." In *Studies on the Seven Sages of Rome, and Other Essays in Medieval Literature Dedicated to the Memory of Jean Misrahi*, edited by Henri Niedzielski, Hans R. Runte and William L. Hendrickson, pp. 7–27. Honolulu: Educational Research Associates, 1978.

Baethgen, Friedrich. *Sindban oder die Sieben Weisen Meister, Syrisch und Deutsch.* Leipzig, 1879.

Benfey, Theodor. "Einige Bemerkungen über das indische Original der zum Kreise der Sieben Weisen Meister gehörigen Schriften." *Mélanges asiatiques tirés du Bulletin de l'Académie Impériale des Sciences de Saint-Petersbourg* 3 (1858): 188ff.

————. *Pantschatantra.* Leipzig, 1899. (Indian origin)

Berne, Mauricette. "Les Versions françaises en prose du *Roman des sept sages.*" Thèse, Ecole Nationale des Chartes (Paris), 1966.

————. "Les Versions françaises en prose du *Roman des sept sages.*" *Positions des thèses soutenues par les élèves de la promotion de 1966 pour obtenir le diplôme d'archiviste paléographe.* Paris: Ecole Nationale des Chartes, 1966.

Brunner, Karl. *The Seven Sages of Rome.* Early English Text Society, o.s. 191. London, 1933. (Southern Middle English version)

Buchner, Georg. *Die "Historia Septem Sapientum" nach der Innsbrucker Handschrift vom Jahre 1342. Nebst einer Untersuchung über die Quelle des "Sevin Sages" des Johne Rolland von Dalkeith.* Erlangen-Leipzig, 1889.

Campbell, Killis. *The Seven Sages of Rome.* Reprint. Geneva: Slatkine, 1975.

————. "A Study of the Romance of the Seven Sages with Special Reference to the Middle English Versions." *PMLA* 14 (1899): 1–107.

Carmoly, Eliakim. *Les Paraboles de Sendabar.* Paris, 1849. (French translation of Hebrew)

Clouston, W. A. *The Book of Sindibad: or, Story of the King, his Son, the Damsel, and the Seven Viziers. From the Persian and Arabic.* Glasgow, 1884.

————. "The Book of Sindibad." *The Athenaeum*, no. 3333 (London, 12 September 1891), 355–56.

Colum, Padraic. "The Six Swans." *Grimm's Fairy Tales.* New York: Random House, 1944, pp. 232–37. (*cygni*)

Comparetti, Domenico. *Ricerche Intorno al Libro de Sindibad.* Milan, 1869.
————. "Virgil im Dolopathos." *Virgil im Mittelalter.* Leipzig, 1975, pp. 201ff. (Trans. Hans Dütschke)
————. *Virgilio nel Medio Evo.* Florence, 1896. (English translation by Benecke, London, 1895)

Constable, F. C., ed. *Philostratus: The Life of Apollonius of Tyana* (Loeb Classical Library, 2), 1912, pp. 8–13. (A later version of the Egyptian lustful stepmother)

Coote, H. C., trans. *Researches Respecting the Book of Sindibad,* by D. Comparetti. London, 1882.

Crosland, J. "*Dolopathos* and the Seven Sages of Rome." *Medium Aevum* 25 (1956): 1–12.

Dégh, Linda. *Folk Tales and Society: Story-Telling in a Hungarian Peasant Community.* Bloomington: Indiana University Press, 1969, pp. 157–58. (*puteus*)

Eberhard, A. *In Johannis de Alta Silva libro qui inscribitur Dolopathos emendationum spicilegium.* Magdeburg, 1875.

Ehret, Ph. *Der Verfasser des versificirten Romans des VII Sages und Herberz, der Verfasser des altfranzösischen Dolopathos.* Dissertation, Heidelberg, 1886.

Epstein, Morris. "The Manuscripts, Printed Editions and Translations of *Mishle Sendebar.*" *Bulletin of the New York Public Library* 63 (1959): 63–87.

————. "*Mishle Sendebar*: New Light on the Transmission of Folklore from East to West." *American Academy for Jewish Research Proceedings* (1958): 1–17.

————. *Tales of Sendebar. Mishle Sindbad. An Edition and Translation of the Hebrew Version of the Seven Sages Based on Unpublished Manuscripts.* Philadelphia: The Jewish Publication Society of America, 1967.

————. "Vatican Hebrew Codex 100 and the *Historia Septem Sapientum.*" *Proceedings of the Fourth World Congress of Jewish Studies* (1965). Jerusalem, 1967.

Gilleland, Brady B. "The *Dolopathos* of Johannes de Alta Silva: A New Evaluation." In *Studies on the Seven Sages of Rome and Other Essays in Medieval Literature Dedicated to the Memory of Jean Misrahi,* edited by Henri Niedzielski, Hans R. Runte and William L. Hendrickson, pp. 32–42. Honolulu: Educational Research Associates, 1978.

————. "Three Stories from the *Dolopathos* of Johannes de Alta Silva." *Allegorica* 2 (1977): 99–117. (*creditor, Polyphemus, cygni*)

Glenn, Justin. "The Polyphemus Folktale and Homer's Cyclopeia." *Transactions of the American Philological Association* 102 (1971): 133–81. (*Polyphemus*)

Goedeke, Karl. "Liber de septem sapientibus." *Orient und Occident* 3 (1866): 385–423. (*Scala Celi*)

Gollancz, Hermann. *The History of Sindban.* London, 1897. (Syriac version)

Gomme, George L., ed. *The History of the Seven Wise Masters of Rome*. London: Villon Society, 1885.

Grimm, W. *Abhandlungen der Berliner Akademie* 1857: 4–7. *(latronis filii; Polyphemus)*

———. *Kinder- und Hausmärchen*, no. 49. ("Six Swans": silence motif) P.

Colum, p. 232.

Gröber, Gustav. *Grundriss der romanischen Philologie*. Strasbourg: Karl J. Trübner, 1893, pp. 605–8. *(Seven Sages)*

———. *Grundriss*, pp. 608–10. (Dolopathos)

Haupt, M. *Altdeutsche Blätter* 1 (Leipzig, 1836): 119 ff. (MS. Leipzig Univ.-Bibl. 1270 of German *Dolopathos*)

Hennecke, E. and Schneemelcher, W. *New Testament Apocrypha* (Translation ed. by R. McL. Wilson), 2 vols. Philadelphia: The Westminster Press, 1963.

Hilka, Alfons. *Historia septem sapientum I*. Heidelberg, 1912. (Fourteenth-fifteenth century Latin translation of Hebrew)

———. *Historia septem sapientum II*. Heidelberg, 1913. *(Dolopathos)*

Holmes, U. T. and Giduz, H. *Les Contes des sept sages*. New York, 1938.

Huet, Gedeon. *Romania* 34 (1905): 206–14. *(cygni)*

———. *Romania* 37 (1908): 162. *(gaza)*

Jaunzems, John. "Structure and Meaning in the *Seven Sages of Rome*." In *Studies on the Seven Sages of Rome and Other Essays in Medieval Literature Dedicated to the Memory of Jean Misrahi*, edited by Henri Niedzielski, Hans R. Runte and William L. Hendrickson, pp. 43–62. Honolulu: Educational Research Associates, 1978.

Johannis de Alta Silva. *Dolopathos*. Reprint. Geneva: Slatkine, (in press).

Keene, D. "The Hippolytus Triangle, East and West." *Yearbook of Comparative and General Literature* 11 (1962): 162–71.

Keller, H.-A. von. *Li Romans des Sept Sages*. Tübingen, 1836. (French verse version K)

Keller, John Esten. *The Book of the Wiles of Women*. Chapel Hill, 1956.

———. *El Libro de los Engaños*. Chapel Hill: University of North Carolina Studies in the Romance Languages and Literatures, 1953.

———. *El Libro de los Engaños*. Revised edition, 1959.

———. "Old Spanish *garpios*." *Hispanic Review* 22 (1954): 228–31.

Kelly, Douglas. "Motif and Structure as Amplification of Topoi in the *Sept Sages de Rome* Prose Cycle." In *Studies on the Seven Sages of Rome and Other Essays in Medieval Literature Dedicated to the Memory of Jean Misrahi*, edited by Henri Niedzielski, Hans R. Runte and William L. Hendrickson, pp. 133–54. Honolulu: Educational Research Associates, 1978.

Köhler, R. *Kleine Schriften* 1, 82–134 *(striges)*; 201–9 *(gaza)*; 211 *(creditor)*.

———. *Kleine Schriften* 2, 380 *(viduae filius)*; 401–5 *(senex)*.

Krappe, A. H. "The Seven Sages." *Archivum Romanicum* 8, 386–407; 9, 345–65; 16, 271–82; 19, 213–26.

Krzyzanowski, Julian. "The Old Polish Version of the 'History of the Seven Sages.'" In *Studies on the Seven Sages of Rome and Other Essays in Medieval Literature Dedicated to the Memory of Jean Misrahi*, edited by Henri Niedzielski, Hans R. Runte and William L. Hendrickson, pp. 79–87. Honolulu: Educational Research Associates, 1978.

Legrand d'Aussy, Pierre-Jean-Baptiste. *Fabliaux ou contes, fables et romans du XIIe et du XIIIe siècle*. Paris: J. Renouard, 1829. 2, 431–32 (*nutrix* ?); 3, 153–55 (*inclusa*); 5, 125–29 (*filius* ?)

Macler, Frédéric. *Contes syriaques: Histoire de Sindban*. Paris, 1903. (French translation of Friedrich Baethgen)

———. *La Version arménienne de l'Histoire des Sept Sages de Rome*. Paris, 1919. (French rendering of Jacob Thokat's Armenian translation of 1614)

McMunn, Meradith T. "Psychological Realism in the *Roman de Kanor*, Last of the *Sept Sages* Continuations." In *Studies on the Seven Sages of Rome and Other Essays in Medieval Literature Dedicated to the Memory of Jean Misrahi*, edited by Henri Niedzielski, Hans R. Runte and William L. Hendrikson, pp. 181–200. Honolulu: Educational Research Associates, 1978.

Manitius, Max and Lehmann, Paul. "Johannes de Alta Silva." In their *Geschichte der lateinischen Literatur des Mittelalters* 3 (Handbuch der Altertumswissenschaft 9, ii, 3), pp. 177–81, 281–82. Munich: Beck, 1931.

Matsubara, Hidéichi. "Chinese and Japanese Versions of *gaza*." In *Studies on the Seven Sages of Rome and Other Essays in Medieval Literature Dedicated to the Memory of Jean Misrahi*, edited by Henri Niedzielski, Hans R. Runte and William L. Hendrickson, pp. 104–8. Honolulu: Educational Research Associates, 1978.

———. "Une Version japonaise de gaza." *Mélanges de langue et littérature françaises du moyen-âge offerts à Pierre Jonin*. Aix-en-Provence: CUER MA, 1979 (Senefiance, 7), pp. 427–36.

Meyer, Paul. *Bulletin de la Société des Anciens Textes Français*, (1896), pp. 71 ff. (MS. B. N. nouv. acq. fr. 934 no. 6 of Herbert's *Dolopathos*)

Misrahi, Jean. *Le Roman des Sept Sages*. Reprint. Geneva: Slatkine, 1975.

———. *Les Sept Sages de Rome*. Paris, 1933. (French verse version K)

Montaiglon, Anatole de and Brunet, Charles. *Le Roman de Dolopathos*. Paris, 1856.

Mussafia, Adolf. "Über die Quelle des altfranzösischen *Dolopathos*." *Sitzungsberichte der philosophisch-historischen Classe der kaiserlichen Akademie der Wissenschaften* (Vienna) 48 (1864): 246–67.

Niedzielski, Henri. "La Formation d'un cycle littéraire au moyen âge: Exemple des *Sept Sages de Rome*." In *Studies on the Seven Sages of Rome and Other Essays in Medieval Literature Dedicated to the Memory of Jean Misrahi*, edited by Henri Niedzielski, Hans R. Runte and William L. Hendrickson, pp. 119–32. Honolulu: Educational Research Associates, 1978.

———. *Le Roman de Helcanus*. Geneva: Droz, 1966.

———. Runte, Hans R.; and Hendrickson, William L., eds. *Studies on the Seven Sages of Rome and Other Essays in Medieval Literature Dedicated to the Memory of Jean Misrahi*. Honolulu: Educational Research Associates, 1978.

Oesterley, Hermann, ed. *Gesta Romanorum*. Berlin, 1872. (no. 124, *senex*; no. 195, *creditor*; p. 458, *nutrix* [?]; pp. 510, 627, 641–45, *filius* [?]; pp. 597, 598, 620, 624, 648, 665, *Cardamum* [?]; p. 681, *assassinus* [?])

———. *Johannis de Alta Silva Dolopathos sive de Rege et Septem Sapientibus*. Strasbourg, 1873.

Ogle, M. B. "The Stag-Messenger Episode." *American Journal of Philology* 37 (1916): 387–416. (*cygni; striga et fons*).

Oldfather, W. A. and Madden, M. "The Urbana Manuscript of *Syntipas*." *Speculum* 2 (1927): 473–75.

Palermo, Joseph. *The Roman de Cassidorus: An Unpublished Continuation of the Roman des sept sages*. New York, 1954.

———. "Le roman des sept sages." *Dictionnaire des Lettres Françaises*. Vol. 1: *Le Moyen Age*. Paris: Fayard, 1964, pp. 656–57.

Paris, Gaston. *Deux Rédactions du Roman des Sept Sages de Rome*. Paris, 1876. (French prose versions D and H)

———. *La Légende de Trajan*. Paris, 1878. (*viduae filius*)

———. [Review of Henry Alfred Todd's edition of *La Naissance du Chevalier au Cygne, ou Les Enfants changés en cygnes*.] *Romania* 19 (1890): 314–40. (*cygni*)

Perry, Ben Edwin. "The Origin of the Book of Sindbad." *Fabula* 3 (1960): 1–94.

———. *Secundus the Silent Philosopher*. Ithaca: Cornell University Press, 1964, pp. 1, 17, 64 on *Sindbād*.

Pieper, M. "Das Schatzhaus des Rhampsinit bei Shakespeare." *Zeitschrift für ägyptische Sprache und Altertumskunde* 68 (1932): 70–71. (*gaza*)

Raby, F. J. E. "The 'Manerius' Poem and the Legend of the Swan-Children." *Speculum* 10 (1935): 68–71.

Rand, E. K. "The Mediaeval Virgil." *Studi Medievali*, n.s. 5 (1932): 418–42.

Ranke, Kurt, ed. *Enzyklopädie des Märchens, Handwörterbuch zur historischen und vergleichenden Erzählforschung*. Berlin-New York, 1975–77. Vol. 1, pp. 350–53 *assassinus*, p. 338 *puteus*, pp. 445–63 *amici*.

Runte, Hans R. "Edition critique du *Roman des sept sages de Rome*: La Tradition manuscrite de la Version A." XIV Congresso Internazionale di Linguistica e Filologia Romanza (Naples, 1974).

108

————. "L'Histoire de la male marastre: Nouvelles Recherches sur le *Roman des sept sages.*" *Actes du XIIIe Congrès International de Linguistique et Philologie romanes* (Quebec, 1971). Quebec: Presses de l'Université Laval, 1973, pp. 215–22.

————. *Li Ystoire de la male marastre: Version M of the Roman des sept sages de Rome.* Beihefte zur Zeitschrift für romanische Philologie, 141. Tübingen: Niemeyer, 1974.

————. "Zur Textgeschichte des Roman des sept sages de Rome: Die zwei Autoren der *Histoire de la male marastre.*" *Neuphilologische Mitteilungen* 75 (1974): 368–76.

Schmidt, Michael. *Neue Beiträge zur Geschichte der Sieben Weisen Meister.* Cologne, 1928.

Sengelmann, Heinrich. *Das Buch von den Sieben Weisen Meistern.* Halle, 1842. (German translation of Hebrew)

Sinseimer, Hermann.*Shylock: The History of a character.* New York: Benjamin Bloom, 1968, pp. 71-82.(*creditor*)

Spargo, John Webster. *Virgil the Necromancer: Studies in Virgilian Legends.* Harvard Studies in Comparative Literature 10. Cambridge, Mass., 1934.

Thorpe, Lewis. "Les 'contes desrimez' et les premiers romans en prose." *Mélanges de langue et de littérature du moyen âge et de la Renaissance offerts à Jean Frappier.* Geneva: Droz, 1970. Vol. 2, 1031–41.

————. "Paulin Paris and the French Sequels to *Les sept sages de Rome.*" *Scriptorium* 2 (1948): 59–68.

————. "Le Roman des sept sages et ses continuations." *Dictionnaire des Letters Françaises.* Vol. 1: *Le Moyen Age.* Paris: Fayard, 1964, pp. 657–58.

————. "Les sept sages de Rome: Un nouveau fragment de manuscrit." *Mélanges Rostaing* (1974), vol. 2, 1143–1247.

Tupper, Frederick and Ogle, Manbury Bladen, trans. *Walter Map: De Nugis Curialium.* London: Chatto and Windus, 1926. Pp. 131-155, the wicked queen; pp. 166-172, the faithless wife; pp. 172-176, the faithless wife; p. 196 the *Aureolus* of Theophrastus as mentioned in *Dolopathos.*

Varnhagen, Hermann. *Eine italienische Prosaversion der Sieben Weisen, nach einer Londoner Handschrift herausgegeben.* Berlin, 1881.

Wesselski. *Mönchslatein.* Leipzig, 1909. (no. 31 *canis*; no. 67 *puteus*; no. 138 *creditor*)

Wikeley, John Keith. "An Italian Version of *The Seven Sages of Rome.*" *News from the Rare Book Room* 16 (December, 1976; University of Alberta), 66–74.

Wright, Thomas, ed. *Alexandri Neckam de naturis rerum.* p. 255. (*senex*)

Yohannan, J. D. *Joseph and Potiphar's Wife in World Literature.* New York: New Directions, 1968.

Index Nominum

mrts

medieval & renaissance texts & studies *is a research program and publication program of CEMERS, the Center for Medieval and Early Renaissance Studies at the State University of New York at Binghamton. The main* mrts *series emphasizes texts, translations, and major research tools. From time to time distinguished monographs and reprints will also be published.* mrts *is also engaged in the adaptation of modern technology for scholarly purposes and in fostering new approaches to scholarly publication.*

Dolopathos: or the King and the Seven Wise Men is here presented in a lively, graceful, and eminently readable first English translation of the twelfth-century text. *Dolopathos*, the earliest extant example of the western branch of *The Seven Sages* cycle, contains three stories of special interest: "The Creditor" embodies the pound-of-flesh theme; "Polyphemus" is a parody on the Cyclops story; and "The Swans" is an early example of the Lohengrin tale. *Dolopathos* is built around the framework of the lustful wife who accuses her stepson of attempted rape. Professor Gilleland traces the geneology of this framework in his introduction, showing its ancient origins in western and eastern writings. The text is important as a medieval working of this framework, with the medieval world view setting it apart from other versions. Although the writer (a Cistercian monk) claims to be illiterate, Professor Gilleland shows that he is clearly a scholar with abundant knowledge of classical literature, history, and philosophy, and with a good grasp of rhetorical devices.

Brady B. Gilleland is a Professor of Classics at the University of Vermont, and was Chairman of that department from 1967-72. He has also been Scholar in Residence at Princeton University and a member of the Advisory Council to the School of Classical Studies of the American Academy in Rome. He is an editor of *English Etymology, Greek & Latin*, with Z. P. Ambrose and R. R. Schlunk (Burlington, Vt., 1979 (and Petronius' *The Satiricon* with E. T. Sage (Appleton-Century-Crofts, 1969).